LEFT OUT

WHEN THE TRUTH DOESN'T FIT IN

a memoir

Tara Reade

foreword by
Rose McGowan

LEFT OUT: *WHEN THE TRUTH DOESN'T FIT IN*
Published by TVGuestpert Publishing
Copyright © 2020 by Tara Reade

ISBN-13: 978-1-7358981-1-7

This publication is designed to provide accurate and authoritative information in regards to the subject matter covered. It is sold with the understanding that the publisher is not engaged in rendering legal, accounting, or other professional service. If legal advice or other expert assistance is required, the services of a competent professional person should be sought. – From a Declaration of Principles

Jointly adopted by a committee of the American Bar Association and a committee of Publishers and Associations.

Some names and identifying details have been changed to protect the privacy of individuals. All brand names, product names, and team names used in this book are trademarks, registered trademarks or trade names of their respective holders.

TVGuestpert Publishing and the TVG logo are trademarks of Jacquie Jordan Inc.
TVGuestpert & TVGuestpert Publishing are subsidiaries of Jacquie Jordan Inc.
TVGuestpert & TVGuestpert Publishing are visionary media companies that seek to educate, enlighten, and entertain the masses with the highest level of integrity. Our full-service production company, publishing house, management, and media development firm promises to engage you creatively and honor you and ourselves, as well as the community, in order to bring about fulfillment and abundance both personally and professionally.

DC Cover Photo by Daniel Hornal
Front Book Cover Design by Avalon Clare Illustration
Author Photos by Darin Hayes Photography
Edited by TVGuestpert Publishing
Special thanks to Avalon Clare for the beautiful book cover

Published by TVGuestpert Publishing

11664 National Blvd, #345
Los Angeles, CA 90064
310-584-1504
www.TVGuestpertPublishing.com
www.TVGuestpert.com
First Printing March 2021
10 9 8 7 6 5 4 3 2 1

LEFT OUT

WHEN THE TRUTH DOESN'T FIT IN

a memoir

TARA READE

*foreword by
Rose McGowan*

DEDICATION

To my daughter, my fellow rainbow hunter, Michaela Rosalie, who brings me so much joy and inspired love;

To my mother, Jeanette, who gave me unending love and an artist's strength to find my own courage.

"My mother wanted me to be her wings, to fly as she never quite had the courage to do. I love her for that. I love the fact she wanted to give birth to her own wings."

- Erica Jong
(One of my mother's favorite authors)

ACKNOWLEDGMENTS

Gratitude practice is something I do every day in either a meditative prayer or thought. There are many people to whom I wish to express my gratitude:

My family. My daughter Michaela, who has dealt with a firestorm and stood with me. Charm and the kitties who remind me daily of unconditional love. My brother Collin and his sweet family, Dani, Piper, Greyson and Violet, whose lives were impacted in seen and unseen ways. My brother Michael, good night Sweet Prince. My brother Brent and his wife Kathy and their family. Anette, who stood by me and cried with me. Maeve, who knew all these years and let me break the silence in my own time. Wendy Dale, Gina and Genae Kindsher (who are always there for Charm and me). Louie, David, and Julie, Heidi, Laura, Joe, Ilene and Cal and the gang, Tara Sutphen who showed me the path. Now I have to take it. Don, who got my story heard. Kait, you brought my mom back for a minute. Lynda LaCasse who has stood by me and been such a good friend for decades, Avalon Clare (my Aaron Rodgers) and Angus. To Rose McGowan, who stands fiercely with me.

The brave journalists Katie Halper, Ryan Grim, Rich McHugh, Russia Today who lifted my voice, Megyn Kelly, Krystal Ball, Amy Goodman, Nathan Robinson, Joseph Wulfson and others. Joseph Backholm, who listened and understood my pain in 2003. Alex, and Vera, and also Lee, who listened and held my grief about what happened in 2012. My lawyer, Daniel Hornal, who got on this bumpy, wild ride. Donnye, who helps in so many ways; hair and makeup is a part of it. Darin Hayes, who gave me the beautiful photos while wrangling horses. Thank you to the TVGuestpert Team, Jacquie Jordan, Stephanie and Laura, for bringing my words to the world.

Gratitude to survivors.

TABLE OF CONTENTS

FOREWORD

What do you call someone who has been silenced, scorned, hated, dismissed, and terrorized by power? I call her a hero for truth. I call her Tara Reade. Many will say Tara wrote this book for profit. And I will say, "So what?" What if your life history had been twisted to suit a narrative that benefits only the DNC, only Joe Biden? What would you do if at every turn you were being smeared for the benefit and convenience of your rapist? Tara's life has been picked apart and disassembled by wealthy and powerful liars—Democrats who want to retain their power at all cost.

What would you do to stop your rapist from becoming one of the most powerful people on earth? Would you go to any length to speak up? Tara would, and Tara has. It takes extraordinary strength and a willingness to take on more trauma. I know this to be true. I also can recognize when a person is severely traumatized as Tara has been. Tara is also a truth-teller. Do you understand the fortitude one must have to be a person who speaks of their deepest pain out loud, only to be scorned? I can tell you the answer to this, it is hell.

By speaking up on behalf of Tara, I have been blackballed by so many, including *The New York Times*, whom I helped win a Pulitzer Prize. Fake news isn't only what's written, it's what's purposely omitted. When it comes to observing the cabal of liberal media titans working against Tara, the only word that comes to mind is sad. I used to believe they were the good guys, just as I used to believe the Democrats were. After one call from Hillary Clinton's spokesman to NBC News executives, an exposé of my own rapist was shut down. I know who is colluding with whom, and why. By witnessing the vitriol aimed at Tara by all too many on the Left, it has cemented for me the fact that they can be just as foul as the worst of those on the Right. The delusion millions of Democrats seem to have is that by being a "liberal," they are exempt from being bad humans. What a long con this two-party system has run on the American public. What a long con people have run on themselves.

For everyone who has gleefully tweeted LOCK HER UP to Tara, I have a message for you: Take a hard look at yourself. YOU are accomplices to evil. For those who question why Tara spoke up only when Biden was the presumptive nominee, you have been lied to. Open your eyes, your ears, and your hearts. Listen to survivors, not just when it's politically convenient. Life is complicated and messy. But, this does not make someone a liar, this makes them complex.

Tara Reade is a hero to me. Read her words and let her be a hero to you too.

—*Rose McGowan*

Actress, Author, Activist

INTRODUCTION

"Words can travel thousands of miles.
May my words create mutual understanding and love.
May they be as beautiful as gems, as lovely as flowers."
—Thich Nhat Hanh.

"My candle burns at both ends; it will not last the night; but ah,
my foes, and oh, my friends; it gives a lovely light."
—Edna St. Vincent Millay

I sat in my car packed beyond its capacity, my cats howling protests from their carriers. My horse was with a professional hauler and had already been an hour on the road. Pandemic, scandal, death threats, harassment, eviction, loss of work—I suddenly felt all my audacity, my fire and my strength, drain from my body. My tears started to slowly fall. Before I pulled out from the driveway, I saw the doe that would come to my little studio rental house month-to-month to peacefully lie near my cat. Wild yet friendly, she would munch on the grass watching me. How many days and nights her quiet presence got me through the chaos. The doe looked confused at my leaving. I had left her carrots and whispered a final goodbye. When I pulled away from the little home, I felt alone and defeated.

After a short drive, I pulled over to check that everything was stable on the roof of the car. This time, I broke down in tears as anxiety flooded my body. I prayed. I prayed for myself, the little doe left behind, my horse, my cats, my family. I thought of my older brother Michael, long departed from this earth, and prayed, "Michael, please send me a sign, let me know what to think." I sighed and looked around. Wild turkeys wobbled past, horses grazed, and I felt a silent breeze.

When I turned my car back on, the lyrics coming from the radio were, *"Mama, don't worry about a thing, every little things gonna be alright…three little birds upon my doorstep… This is my message to you woo hoo…"* I laughed through my tears. "Three Little Birds" by Bob Marley was the song playing when my daughter was born. I will never forget looking into her eyes and feeling a love and devotion beyond any I had ever experienced. Michaela coming into the world was the most joyous and sacred event of my life, which has been filled with difficulties. I took a deep breath and smiled as I thought of Michael and how he would have loved my daughter had he been alive.

I whispered, "Got it, Michael," to the heavens, and resumed my journey to a new home.

I wrote this book for my daughter, my family, your daughter, your sister, your friends, your mother and grandmother, for all the men in our lives, and you. This story has little to do with justice and more to do about healing from pain. My story has traumatic events but also joyous moments.

My book and the stories from my life create the tapestry of connections, positive and negative, that ultimately form a narrative that many women experience in their professional and personal lives. This book is a compilation of some of my opinions and memories. I protected certain people who did not want to be in the public by changing names and circumstances. Even if you know who they are, let them be. It's my story, not theirs.

This is not an attack on any political party. I have said often that I was a lifelong Democrat, and my work choices have reflected that commitment. However, the very people I supported and worked for all my life abandoned me. The stunning weaponization of class shaming and fear by the mainstream media to try to silence me has been deplorable. I was pushed aside in political interest and left out of any conversations. I hope to evoke change so that other survivors do not have to feel the pain of isolation and rejection simply because they spoke out against a powerful person. There were many people on my path who provided inspiration and love to me, without giving a second thought to establishing my credibility or the veracity of my story, but simply because they cared. There are some things that happen which we cannot control, but we can control how we respond.

As I wrote this, my daughter experienced a huge betrayal when social media trolls sought out her father (from whom she is estranged and who has no parental rights after they were legally terminated). Her father fed these trolls false information about her and stalked her again. These trolls posted misinformation about her and her life, prompting her to create a video pleading for her father and the trolls to leave her alone. Fortunately, she is a strong and positive person. I am in awe of her calm and rational approach to problems all while she is still only in her twenties. One of the things she shared with me was that she is proud of me. That means so much, as I feared my public statements about what happened in 1993 made her life worse. Instead, she has told me she feels good about my coming forward.

One message I tried to convey is that moving from victim to survivor is not a linear process and takes effort. Whatever happens in our lives and the problems we endure, the traumas and successes that make up our experiences do not define us. We can choose to define the experience. In March of 2019, I started my journey publicly discussing Joe Biden. Finally, in 2020, when Joe Biden was possibly going to drop from the presidential race, I spoke out about my full history.

I have been asked many times if I regret coming forward, given the vitriol that I have received. I have been left out of any national conversation, including the #MeToo movement, which the Democrats quickly dropped as their mantle once it no longer served their party's narrative. No, to answer that question regarding regret, I do not regret coming forward. The social media trolls, paid and unpaid by the campaigns, harassing my family and me, the media bias against me, all of it says more about the patriarchy of America and the way rape culture has been institutionalized to protect powerful men from any accountability than it does about me.

I have observed in my case and other cases how the Democratic National Committee enables and empowers sexual predators. The DNC has now weaponized mobs of social media trolls and troll farms to attack individual American citizens who it sees as a threat. At what point does the collective witnessing of sexual harassment and misconduct by a powerful person, and silencing of the survivor, make the DNC complicit to sexual violence? When one looks at our two political parties, they are not only complicit, they are rewarding the predators with the blessing of more powerful positions. It is unconscionable that a political organization is allowed to use its resources to attack survivors, or anyone, on a personal level, just because they have opposing views.

No political party gets a pass. Sexual violence is a non-partisan issue. I would say to other survivors that I came forward during a perfect storm of barriers that tried to prevent my truth from coming into the light. I do not wish to place blame, but rather to reveal those who participated in my silencing, so that we can all learn for the future.

I do know if you are choosing to stand and tell your own story to the world, be ready for the denials and name-calling to be thrown your way. They feel like glass shards ripping into your psyche and tearing at the very seams of your heart. Be ready to stand in that firestorm and speak into the void. You may lose everything and gain nothing. Personally, I do not regret one minute or one conversation I have had because this has all brought a deeper learning. I would also advise you to know your rights, and know that conditions for employment should not silence you about sexual misconduct.

I experienced deep relief by not keeping the secret for a powerful man. Speak out, be steadfast with truth and your own sense of self, but know you will be tested to your very core. The reward is existential yet complete. The freedom to speak truth to power creates an invincible sanctuary for your soul.

CHAPTER I

Tara-rized: Scandal in a Pandemic

"May you have an interesting life."
—Chinese blessing and curse

There is a beach in Morro Bay, CA, where I used to ride my dappled grey Arabian horse, Charizmaa. When her hooves pounded the sand, her lope made me feel like I was floating. I would lean forward and drop my hands down, brushing the surf with my fingers, skimming the foamy wetness of the waves, as Charizmaa stretched her stride. Our mutual trust was so complete that I could relax into the ride completely. This singular memory carried me through years of struggle and grief.

The day before I left for Washington, D.C. in 1993, I struggled to say goodbye to Charizmaa as I brushed her mane and fed her treats. I knew it would be months before I could see and ride her again. I felt the fluttering of my unknown future pulling at me as I prepared to pack. I had just landed a position with Senator Joseph Biden as a Staff Assistant. I could not have known that what I anticipated as the beginning of a new career would turn out to be the end.

April 2020

Years later, I stood staring out my kitchen window at a mother turkey with her babies trailing and beeping behind her. The neighbor's wisteria was beginning to fade in the spring. I methodically ground my coffee for the pour over, savoring the nutty smell, my cats demanding their food -- when my trance was broken by my phone buzzing then ringing at the counter. My daughter's name popped up, so I answered it.

"Mom... Mama... I can't, oh my god... have you seen?" my daughter, Michaela, incoherently shrieked out from the other end of the phone.

I had not yet turned on the radio or looked at the Internet that day, and I did not own a TV.

"Mom, they are talking about you and... oh my god... they... it's..." she was sputtering in a high pitch that she used when she was angry.

"Hold on, Michaela, what is going on?" I remained calm.

"People online and in the media are calling you names and a liar!" She was on the verge of tears. "I keep getting calls and messages on my phone asking for you."

I gazed out the window as I listened to her on speaker. The mother turkey was now herding the smallest baby away from the driveway. I watched her weave and expertly keep her little flock together.

I reluctantly looked at my twitter feed and the flood of articles on the Internet. Liar, Bitch, Whore and worse were scattered throughout my direct messages and emails.

"Kiks, we knew this might get difficult." Kiks is my special nickname for Michala.

"Difficult?! Ma, this is unreal what they are saying about you. Are you okay?"

I replied, "Give me a minute, sweets, and I will call you back."

"Okay," she responded sadly.

I sighed as I told her how much I loved her before I hung up. My history with Joe Biden that had once been a secret between my family and me, along with a few select friends, was now fodder for the world.

Later that morning, a strident female voice with an East Coast twang called.

"Tara?" she asks.

I answered "Yes?"

"This is Beth Reinhard from *The Washington Post*. You have come forward with a sexual assault allegation against Joe Biden. Don't you realize this will hurt his campaign?" She is almost shouting at me.

I was stunned and silent for a second. I had talked to reporters before, including *The Post* in 2019, when I discussed the sexual harassment I endured in Joe Biden's office. However, this was the first time I was scolded. She continued her questions that sounded more like statements. I stayed on the phone to answer all of them.

"I was too scared to come forward with everything, and I have been trying to come forward for a while!" I sounded defensive even to myself.

She launched into a demand to hear my entire story.

"I spoke about it all on the Katie Halper podcast." I answered with a sigh.

"I need to hear it from the beginning from you," she insisted.

I am not in the entertainment business. I'm a "civilian" to the media, and I did not realize that it's entirely plausible to say "no" to reporters or not respond at all. At this particular moment, I had no public relations guidance and no lawyer. I thought it may be poor form to not answer, even impolite. Also, I was isolated in my studio house, like most of the country, in the middle of the Covid-19 pandemic crisis. Sheltering and isolating were still new terms in our collective lexicon—with a very uncertain future to come.

As I started telling her my memory of what happened with Joe Biden, Beth continued to interject, abruptly at times.

As I approached recounting the assault, my emotions swirled, and I felt that dizzying dread wash over me. I hadn't told the story too many times; in fact, I'd spent most of my life trying to erase it and its effect on my whole self.

"Did he move his hand upwards?" she asked.

I felt a sharp intake of my own breath. *What does she mean?* I wondered.

Finally, in a more assertive tone, Beth asked, "Did he touch your clitoris?"

I stammered as I acknowledged he had moved his hand upwards after he pulled out his fingers. *Was she implying that I experienced pleasure? Or was she trying to make it sound consensual? What did this even mean?* She repeated her question, which I heard as an echo.

The conversation ended with my sobbing. "Oh, Tara. I will call you back," she stated impatiently in that discernable Eastern affect. She hung up. There was a double click as she disconnected.

I went to my bathroom and retched. I had not eaten, so I mostly was dry-heaving. I knelt and cried on the bathroom floor. My cat wandered in, his little nose touched me with concern. I picked him up and held him tight until he finally wiggled free from the intensity of my emotions.

Is this how reporters talk? Was this normal for them to cause more traumas with interviews? Why was she asking me about my clitoris? I felt ashamed by my lack of courage to put her in her place and to back off.

Not too long after, I realized why she was asking. I watched as the strange conversations began to unfold on social media.

Later the same day, I found myself on the phone with another reporter asking for my opinion.

Then I came across this tweet from one of the reporters I spoke with:

Richard N Komi
@KomiRichard

Judging by the position of the female vagina, it will not be easy for anyone to just put their finger into the vagina unless their is some Cooperation from the female herself. That is why I believe Tara Reade's allegations is false. She is looking for attention.

9:44 AM · 5/1/20 · Twitter for Android

3 Retweets

I read and reread the offensive post. I read many responses to the awful post. I started to feel numb, as my private parts had now become public discussion and debate.

"Mom, are you doing okay? I saw the latest," Michaela asked during another phone call.

"No... Yes, I am trying to move though this, but wow!" I replied.

"I just cannot believe they are discussing you in this way." She sounded incredulous and angry.

I decided to lighten the conversation, "Well, I guess that man in the article claims he is an expert on consent-based positions, like a vagina whisperer or something." I laughed at the absurdity of my own joke.

I received horrified silence from Michaela, who soon broke her own silence to remind me, "Mom, you are using humor as a defense mechanism again. You need to process this trauma." Wise beyond her young age.

"It is only a mechanism if you laugh," I answered, and Michaela finally chuckled. "Anyway, honey, I know this is super cringe."

"Mom, don't say cringe," she interrupted.

I laughed, remembering her as a teenager scolding me or rolling her eyes at friends when I said things like "lame" or "sketch," as if they were still popular expressions.

"Quit trying to be cool, Mom," she would say as I took her to school.

"Perhaps my vagina wanted to say something to the world," I said philosophically.

"Oh, MY GOD, Mom. THAT is cringe. Do not say the word vagina before coffee." She finally laughed, and the tension and sadness evaporated.

I made a mental note, adding that word to my forbidden-terms list.

"Have you heard from Collin?" she asked me about my younger brother.

"Yes, he didn't know what to say, and he's absorbed in the new stay-at-home guidance. His gigs are cancelling out through June," I responded.

"Wow," Michaela answered.

"Love you, honey."

"Love you, Mama, I have to go to work. Call me later."

For all my bravado and jokes, I was deeply humiliated by the posts and articles. None of the recent events felt amusing. It all brought to the surface the deep and painful trauma that I had denied for a very long time. However, I also did not want to stay in a perpetual state of angst. I wanted to come forward with dignity, and the reality was that I felt quite undignified.

I went to sit outside my little studio house, thankful for the quiet and the nature all around me. The old doe I call Babushka, with white hair around her face, walked near me as I scattered carrots on the ground for her. She is wild and timid. With her wise eye fixed on me, she lay down quietly at the fence, demonstrating her trust while munching on the snack. I set down my phone and deeply breathed in the warm air. Feeling the deer's quiet presence always soothed me in the morning. My cat lay down by my legs while also staring at the deer. I braced myself for the coming days.

CHAPTER 2

Suicidal Thoughts and Other Side Effects

"When you come to the end of your rope, tie a knot and hang on."
—Franklin Roosevelt

There should be a warning label for coming forward about a powerful man. The warning label should read, as follows:

Side effects: May cause loss of job, housing, career, relationships, and suicidal thoughts. Invokes death threats from others; triggers irrational craving for cheese curds, chocolate, and other comfort foods; oh and, causes depression.

A *New York Times* reporter almost killed me. Not on purpose maybe, but she picked up where Beth Reinhard of *The Washington Post* left off trying to destroy my credibility. Lisa Lerer of *the NYT* used her personality to gain my trust, then betrayed both my daughter and me in the most horrible way. Let me explain.

It was late. I sat drinking water in the hot, arid night, as the bright moonlight fell into the skylight, illuminating my room. I listened to the frogs and crickets sing, as I tried to will myself back to sleep. My cats snoozed and shifted drowsily as I tossed. The major media outlets were using me as target practice with headlines daily, calling me "manipulative," "lying," "user," and "I do not believe Tara Reade" opinions from notable feminists.

I curled up in the fetal position imagining friends and family reading every horrible word of these articles, and I felt so lonely, my heart actually ached with pain. I was considered *persona non-grata* by an entire country. I was not just inconvenient, I was collectively hated, dismissed, and despised for coming forward. *The NYT* set the tone with three consecutive and increasingly ugly articles tearing me apart from the age of seven to adulthood in an effort to discredit me. It almost worked, until it didn't. According to the major media outlets, I was to be ignored or smeared—period.

I stared at my skylight trying to absorb the intensity of what had happened while drifting into an uneasy, fretful sleep, remembering the first major article in the *NYT*.

At midnight, my phone buzzed and rang. As a mother, I always answer my phone to make sure my daughter is safe. She is grown and living on her own, but I am always at-the-ready in case she needs me.

I rolled over in my bed to reach the cell phone without looking at the caller ID, "Hello?"

A deep male voice answered, "Traitor."

"What?"

"Fucking traitor."

My email and social media alerts were all going off.

"I know where you live, and I am coming to kill you."

The phone went silent. It was my first official death threat. The article about Biden had posted less than three hours ago to the Associated Press wire. I was still not fully awake as I put on the lights, went to the kitchen and started making tea. For some reason, I like to make tea during a crisis, as if a normal activity can keep the crisis at bay. I looked at my alerts: an email threatening me, tweets and Instagram messages calling me a Russian agent. I sat awake in the middle of the night wondering about the recent events, and how I got here.

Startled by my next cell phone ring, Maeve, a friend of mine called, "*The NYT* printed your social security number that was on your Congressional ID picture. You need to get them to take this down, Tara," she said in one breath instead of her usual slow southern drawl. It was 6am Pacific Time and the article had been up for hours.

I looked at the online article and cried out, "Oh, no!"

I sent a text right away to Lisa Lerer, *the NYT* reporter who had spoken to me. She texted back immediately that she would look into it. The online article blocked out my number, but not before it was screen-shotted and sent to me by strangers on social media. As I fixed my coffee, stretched, and fed the cats,

I was on the phone trying to figure out how to protect myself from fraud…and worse.

But I just wanted to go back to bed and start over. So I dropped the phone.

Lisa Lerer was nice and normal sounding. My first and last mistake was to trust her. Ever. At that point, I was open and earnestly trying to convey my history with Joe Biden. But as article after negative article came out, I began to lose any trust I might have originally had in her. Betrayal by someone with whom you have shared a most difficult trauma cuts deep. Somehow the shared experience of implicit bias should translate to an understanding. However, it would not be the first or last betrayal. A former coworker I had known for years lied about me to the press. When I asked her why, her answer was that we did not need Trump for president again. The election cycle continued to bring the worst out of the feminist movement with its complicit silence or outright damnation of me.

Lisa always came off as reasonable and cajoling. "Oh Tara, I know you are not a Russian agent." Yet, in all three articles it is referenced that I am, as if I may have some weird connection with Russia.

My daughter talked with Lisa and wanted to trust her. After the article, my daughter called me weeping, "Mama, I am so sorry! This is not you, and they did not even talk about you the way I described, except to say you were too poor to afford law books."

"I know, they make me sound like a piece of shit starting from my childhood on," I answered.

My daughter continued, "I texted Lisa about how she is the reason women do not come forward—because of how they are treating you."

Michaela was sobbing. I felt guilty that my trauma from years ago was now hurting her and ruining her day.

I got other calls from relatives and friends upset and incredulous. Collin was silent. My brother had warned me. He was right, to a point. However, *The NYT* article could have been much worse. I protested through my lawyer to *The NYT*, requesting they retract or change blatant lies. They neither agreed to, nor did they offer any help to resolve the issues they caused by having published my social security number. The media outlets knew I did not have the resources for an expensive lawsuit and took full advantage of the fact.

THE NYT HEADLINE: Examining Tara Reade's Sexual Assault Allegation Against Joe Biden

Liberal activists, journalists, and Democratic politicians slammed me. The betrayals by celebrities or politicians were stunning; but the personal betrayals from friends and some family were far more painful. People would ask me the same questions over and over as if it would change what happened in 1993. Why didn't you come forward during Obama/Biden? I answered many times that I voted for Obama, and Biden just happened to be on the ticket. There was no platform then such as #MeToo, and my daughter was young; we still had to keep a low profile. There was also this part of me that wondered if Joe Biden had at all changed through the years, and I stayed in this profound denial for a long time. Whenever I did tell some people in my life, I was cautious and kept it vague. It was not until 2019 and Lucy Flores that I knew Biden had not changed at all.

This went on for weeks, I woke up to early east coast reporters on a deadline, who mostly wanted to do hit pieces. I got into what one might consider abusive relationships with them, trying to appease them while walking on proverbial verbal eggshells. After a few weeks, the negative hits begin to wear on me. I lost all confidence and hope. Friends and family stopped calling completely, except for my daughter and Collin.

One night, it all just became too much. I sat on the floor in the corner in silence, a formless shadow. I sensed a nebulous it near me, as I tried to push through the days and the interviews. And it lurked.

"You are nothing, see? Everyone hates you. You are a liar, a manipulator. They say you do not belong here or anywhere." It sneered and added, "But there is a solution." It then slithered away.

I called my brother Collin, and simply said, "Hi."

He said, "Hi" back, against the din of the usual chaos of kids and music in the background.

"Hey, I am having one of the minute-to-minute days," I say, knowing it hears me.

This was code that I would use with my brother, to signal that I wanted help, or at the very least, reassurance. I called him on days like this when I did not want to exist.

In 2019, when most people were afraid of Covid, I was afraid of *it*. *It* came out when I - along with seven other women - came forward about Joe Biden. The media brushed me away, calling me a Russian agent, and *it* just laughed.

"I'm here," Collin replied, "I love you."

One of his children let out a shriek on the other end of the line.

I smiled, as I needed to hear his voice, and I said, "Oh, let's talk later."

Collin asked, "Are you okay?" then quickly apologized for his lack of availability in the moment, "Sorry."

His daughter screamed again. He said, "I will call you back."

I sat quietly. I remembered a quote from Susan Ariel Rainbow Kennedy, whose pen name is SARK, about fear and anxiety, and about a metaphor inviting these feelings in for tea where they can be discussed through yourself.

I decided to try this with my suicidal thoughts. I am not suicidal, I reminded myself, but I am in despair, and I am being publicly punished for speaking out against Biden. I lit incense, said a prayer, meditated, pictured these thoughts, and rationally spoke to them. I fell asleep. When I awoke, my cat was staring at me with a smile. I knew I had chased away the darkness for now. It was gone. However, the hits kept coming.

By the third *NYT* article, I knew it was going to get uglier, as the attacks continued. The press likes to play the game of omission. They omitted my supporters' interviews, accomplishments, praise, and successes. They amplified the negative online rumors about unhappy landlords, debt, bankruptcy, and divorce. They even shamelessly wrote blatant lies and amplified the voices of bottom-feeders. They implied I was a poor, incompetent, uneducated liar since the time I was a kid, and they all but called me a Russian agent, or at least suggested that I had a Russian boyfriend.

In reality, I did not have a boyfriend, imaginary, Russian, or online. I did not change my story or lie about being sexually assaulted. I did not lie about my education. It did not matter, however, because the world now saw me only through the eyes of how *the NYT* portrayed me. I got calls, emails, and death threats calling me a traitor.

I had to file a sheriff's report after my pets were threatened. My daughter received scary calls in the night and demands from private investigators. It was a barrage of unmitigated hate. I clung to any positive messages, as if my whole being depended on them. One Twitter account sent me forty-five pages of threats, more than 11,000 in one month. It was called the Biden Brigade.

All of this was done to hurt me and to silence me.

It almost did silence me...*forever.*

I fell apart.

Lisa Lerer called with her soft prim accent and subtly sanctimonious tone, as she "walked" me "through the story." Those words set off danger alarms in my head and gave me a sinking feeling in my stomach, as I had learned what "I will walk you through your portion of the story" really meant. Yet, I was always astounded by the vitriol *the NYT* was writing about me. Lisa was angry because the questions being asked by *the NYT* were posted publicly by actress and advocate Rose McGowan, who was one of the first women to speak out about sexual harassment against movie producer Harvey Weinstein, in order to show the type of tabloid hit-piece questions they were.

After hanging up with Lisa, I felt the collective weight of the past few weeks descend upon me, so I called Collin.

"Collin!" I literally screamed his name.

"*The NYT* reporter said you never called back. *What the fuck?* Everyone is throwing me under the bus. My own stepbrother, Scott, implied I was lying and spoke badly about me?" I was sobbing this and barely able to get the words out.

"Tara, I told you after I was misquoted by the media and my words twisted. I want nothing more to do with talking publicly. They will just twist my words again. I am with the kids and we are going out," he said, quite obviously frustrated over the whole matter.

"Collin, just call Lisa back. It's awful what they are writing." I said miserably.

I know I should have just left it alone and let him off the hook for the call. However, he did answer Lisa Lerer; Collin was right, it was just a hit piece. No truth was written. Not one of my finest moments. Although I managed to survive being raked over and having my reputation destroyed, it eventually led to losing my work and my housing.

Reporters love the quick pithy gotchas. And they'd hurl them at me, demanding more detail. The national media needs to be trauma-informed. They need to educate themselves on the dynamics of sexual violence and trauma before they interview survivors. They obviously need to work on this, because right now they're terrible at it.

Anthony Zenkus, an adjunct faculty trauma expert with Columbia University and Delphi University stood out from all my steadfast supporters, and still does to this day. He told me that when it comes to the national arena, when powerful men are accused, it's not about telling the real story; it's simply about weaving cherry-picked "facts" into a narrative. And if victims are harmed in the process...oh well. After we talked about the media and what happened, he was refreshingly direct. "Tara, what you're describing about how Joe Biden hurt you, it is a trauma memory. I've taught judges, police, prosecutors and mental health professionals about this.

"When you talk about how you couldn't get the chemical smell, like dry-cleaning, out of your nose, and how you tried to wash it out with soap when you took a shower later that day, that's very typical for sexual assault survivors. The sense of smell is closely linked to trauma memories," Anthony explained.

He continued, "It's common for victims to forget details like exact dates, times or specific locations of their sexual assault. Trauma memories are stored differently in the brain than regular memories.

"You might have been chased by a vicious dog on your way home from school when you were eleven. You may not remember the day of the week it happened, or the street you were on, but you will definitely remember the red car you jumped up on to get away from the dog and the yellow house it was in front of.

"I didn't know what to make of the allegations against Joe Biden when I first heard of them. Then I sat down and listened to your interview on the Katie Halper podcast. When you began speaking about your sexual assault, I just stopped. It was clear that you were speaking from a trauma memory. I thought *these were things I've taught to professionals for years, and this woman is speaking just like every other trauma survivor I've worked with.* My god, I thought, she's telling the truth."

Anthony went on to say, "I have never in all my life seen a survivor treated this way. It's insane. I hope it never happens to anyone again."

Anthony and I talked a bit more and he put me at great ease.

I remembered a phone conversation with Juanita Broderick, who stated she was raped by Bill Clinton after volunteering for him. She describes the brutal attack in her book, *Put Some Ice on That*, which is what Bill Clinton had advised after giving her a black eye. She told me she believed me.

Juanita also said, "You do not owe anybody anything or any explana-tion. He did this. You are brave to speak out."

Juanita was a reminder of the hypocrisy of the Democrats. They continue to use #MeToo to shield their complicit behavior, enabling predators in the highest positions of the party. I have always said the Democratic National Committee and Joe Biden are wolves in sheeps' clothing.

I called Anthony, frustrated that I could remember the "coldness of the wall, but not the exact date or location."

"Why, Anthony, can't this precise information help? I am only saying what I remember. I remember the wall, the smell, the bang on the knee and the shooting pain," I trailed off... frustrated.

Did I think Lisa Lerer or Jim Rutenberg at *the NYT* recognized their bias or cruelty toward me? No. I just don't think they cared that they misrepresented my life and destroyed my reputation to protect the status quo. I do know that Lisa Lerer will not be able to look her own daughter in the eye for the ugly way she treated my story to protect a powerful man.

She used her position to kick someone who was already down—and hurt— just to run cover for a U.S. Senator. Well, I can look at my daughter with confidence, knowing I tried my best to get us out of poverty, and that I stood up for myself. In the end, *the NYT* did not deserve my story or my time.

What I learned is that #BelieveAllWomen is a hashtag that did not include me because I accused a Democrat. What I learned about myself is that I can stand up to a powerful man and his public relations machine. Some survivors are not so fortunate.

Later in the summer of 2020, two survivors of sexual assault from prominent cases committed suicide. I thought of these two young women in their twenties with their whole lives ahead of them. They ended their lives due to cyber bullying and rejection from their community.

I spoke to Louise Godbold, the Executive Director and founder of Echo Training. Louise is also a silence-breaker who came forward about Harvey Weinstein. Lou, as everyone called her, had recently been featured in a documentary about Harvey Weinstein, recounting her own experience with him and the trauma. She has had trauma-informed training and spoke with me about my experiences and about trauma in general.

"Tara? This is Lou. How are you today?" Lou's crisp English accent, sweet and gentle, soothed my frayed nerves.

"Hi, I am not doing so well today," I replied candidly.

"Okay, I am here. Anything you want to talk about right now?" she asked.

"First, I want to say, I am not suicidal, but I am having dark thoughts about not wanting to be here. I also saw that two survivors killed themselves. I don't know. I lost housing. I can't get more work, and people I know will not even return my calls."

"That is a lot." Lou was patient.

"What are your thoughts on all this?" I asked, hoping for sage advice.

Lou explained it to me the following way. Shame is experienced in the same part of the brain as pain. Why would we have this very powerful emotion? We as a species needed to operate in groups for survival, and shame is a way to control members of the group. It causes great pain, so we all avoid triggering shame. However, shame is not the way to educate.

She explained that there is the survival brain, which just controls the senses and is much like the young brain of a two-year-old. It is at a very primitive level. The next level is the emotional part of the brain, where collaboration and understanding are a part of feelings. The thinking brain is the higher brain. When we experience fear, it lights up the amygdala, and that means the thinking brain and you are emotionally regulating. It allows us to accept new situations. Trauma reminders or triggers take charge, and the amygdala is weakened. For instance, children who have been abused react negatively to even a neutral face. Their amygdala is so weakened that a neutral face is still recognized as a threat. As a result of trauma, a lot of the experiences induce reaction from the amygdala part of the brain. Most memories are in the higher part of the thinking brain. Trauma memories are similar to childhood memories in that they are fragmented and disjointed, not very coherent. Odd things will stick out. However, chronological memory is not always accessible. Coherent narratives, like speaking about the trauma or doing art or writing, allows the memory to make sense in the non-linear, non-critical thinking part of the brain. Think of it like taking a shard of glass that is a survival memory and it becomes shaped by this like seaglass, smoother with more chronological order and nuance.

Lou and I talked frankly about the media bias and that Anita Dunn of the Time's Up movement now worked for Biden. Lou was sad to hear the news that Time's Up had not helped me. Lou had a way of putting the science about trauma in such a way that I felt less isolated and realized my experience of this shame and fear is a shared human experience. Later, as I sat with my horse, Charm, in his pasture, feeding him a carrot, I realized the conversation made me feel stronger. As dusk fell, my usual sense of unease about what nighttime would bring set in.

I remembered all the support, but also the women who did not make it. At night, when my world was consumed by despair, I thought of how I almost joined them. *Why was I so lucky to have not succumbed?* I did not know. However, my heart is always with anyone driven to this dark place, and cornered by the thought that the only way to free oneself from pain and hurt is by death. In the end, I hope other survivors receive better treatment and at least the benefit of the doubt, without having their very beings stripped down to nothing, in other people's search, allegedly, for truth.

The next morning, I went back to see Charm. I smelled the horse and his mane. He stood with me silent and motionless, and finally rested his head on my shoulder. I cried for all the pains I had and all the names I was called. I cried for my daughter and the instability that this had caused her. I cried for the pain of all those other young survivors, and I cried for the survivors who couldn't make it to the next day. Charm stood and sighed in a way that made me laugh through tears. As I rubbed his mane and his back, I felt a surge of joy to be alive, love for him, and a feeling of hope, despite all the sorrow. I had survived one of my darkest days.

LEFT OUT: WHEN THE TRUTH DOESN'T FIT IN

CHAPTER 3

The Vultures

"There is no hunting like the hunting of man, and those who have hunted armed men long enough and liked it, never care for anything else thereafter."

—Ernest Hemingway

On a cold spring night in 2019, following a writing group meeting where we had just read each other's pieces, I decided to let the publisher of a local paper know about my real experience with Joe Biden. My chapter had been from a novel I was writing titled, *The Last Snow Tiger*. There were some political scenes in it. One in particular was about a very powerful Senator acting badly. Afterwards, as we walked on the crisp night to our cars, I revealed to a friend that I had been sexually harassed by Biden. I described the harassment I received in the office when I tried to report it, and that I lost my job and career. I hesitated to share the sexual assault. My friend was a publisher of a local newspaper and I was not sure if it was safe.

He said quietly, "Tara, would you be open to talking to one of my reporters?"

I agreed. From writing class, I knew him to be a careful and thoughtful person and one who I could trust.

The reporter called, left a message, and then called again. I answered his second call. This was about to be the first time I spoke publicly about it to anyone. I had told my mom and brother, a best friend at the time, and a few more people over the years. But I never spoke of it in public. There was no #Me-Too or "safe spaces" to discuss it in the '90s (not that it's any easier for survivors to come forward now.)

I described my experience from the beginning.

"It wasn't sexual though, was it?" asked the reporter.

The touching he referred to was by Biden.

I remembered his fingers caressing my neck under my hair and the scared sick feeling about what to do, so I froze.

Silence.

"No. I mean, no, of course not." I traced my fingers down my coffee cup as my throat choked up.

I couldn't do it. I could not tell the whole history. I rationalized that I could eventually get there, but something scared me, something froze inside me, and I shut down.

It was not the reporter, and I don't want to blame him. It was me. Fear snatching away my ability to come forward. The fact of the matter is that all my fears about coming forward had come true, and worse.

My first public conversation about the sexual harassment had been with Lisa Lerer, from *the NYT*. I had discussed my outrage about Biden and the other women. Lisa had put me at ease and was very calm. Our conversations continued.

Laura McGann, editorial director of Vox.com, was calling and courting me to go on record. She was working to get proof that I worked for Biden. Biden's office didn't make this easy. They began by denying my existence. I was able to get my payroll record of service, but not my personnel file, which had vanished. Through a labyrinth of calls to different federal agencies, I was able to speak to someone at an archive for Senate records.

He answered and chuckled, "You're probably never gonna find that file. It is long gone."

I assumed by his demeanor that he had seen the press regarding my experiences with Biden.

My conversations with Laura from Vox.com and Lisa from *the NYT* were always friendly and on a first-name basis, and I developed a trust in both of them - something I would later regret.

I spoke in person to an Associated Press reporter and was resolute upon telling the whole history. However, when he showed up with a middle-aged man wanting to video record me on his cell phone, I lost the courage to speak, and probably minimized the account when I did speak. In fact, I thought to myself, there were witnesses to the sexual harassment and a paper trail of my complaint. The sexual assault? To my knowledge no one saw it or reported it at the time. And by the time of this conversation with the AP, I was already being called a Russian agent.

Later, in May of 2019, I decided to try to talk to Lisa about it. I emailed her and called her. She did not return my call or email. In the ensuing months, I would call and email political public figures, too, all against a backdrop of the ever-present Twitter troll storm. I emailed *The New Yorker* magazine and writer Ronan Farrow three times. I tried contacting others. When no one responded, I confess a part of me was relieved. I could still tell myself I tried. Then in January, 2020, I decided to reach out to Time's Up. The fiasco of trying to come forward went into warp speed.

I took to Twitter several times to state that I had something more to say. A well-known comedian responded in a private message, and we spoke on the phone. It was a week before everyone's life changed due to Covid-19, and began the lock down for the pandemic. She came to my house, and I fixed a vegan meal that she ate voraciously, hungry from a long drive. I told her my entire history with Biden. She looked at some of my paperwork and visited with me for about two hours. "Chloe" could not be named in any articles going forward, as she was worried about her career and the backlash. I understood.

She asked if I would talk to Ryan Grimm, the Intercept's D.C. Bureau Chief, or with podcaster, Katie Halper. I agreed because I knew of their work. Ryan called me and asked about the experiences with Biden and also about the experience with Time's Up.

Katie called, "Hi, is this Tara Reade?"

"Yes," I answered.

"Hi there, wow, I have been reading about your story. I heard from our friend that you may be willing to come on my show," she said with a lilt in her voice to indicate it was a question.

I answered in the affirmative; I liked the fact that she was independent from the network.

She had a charming New York accent that I found delightful and a humorous easygoing approach to guests. In my case, she asked for details. As I articulated the events regarding Biden, she said, "I bet you are getting a ton of calls to appear."

"Not really," I answered.

We made plans to talk again and record the interview. I remember the moment she started recording the show and hearing the click. It felt like I was stepping onto a rollercoaster the way my stomach dropped and fluttered. I drew a sharp breath and began recounting my memories.

I successfully recorded the podcast interview with Katie Halper.

Katie urged me to speak about something Biden said. I remember the lump in my throat as I described him calling me "nothing."

That phrase and the way he pointed his finger at me stayed with me for decades. It echoed my deepest fear about myself, that I was, in fact, nothing. Katie was kind and reached out after the interview to check on me. It was a hard thing. I had just spoken about a secret I had kept since my twenties, and knew the repercussions would affect my whole life.

About a week or two after the Katie Halper podcast "Democracy Now and Rising," I got a text from Laura at Vox. Laura was angry that she lost the scoop, and she let me know it.

Lisa had a different take. "I knew it. I knew there was something more," Lisa stated this publicly and in a broadcast also confirming I had tried to reach back out.

For her part, Laura just wanted to prove me a liar under the guise of investigative journalism. After all, the scoop should have been hers, and she let me know in several conversations, how irritated she was with me. The more she expressed this, the more I shut down. Every conversation with her felt like a battle. If I refused to talk to her, there was the looming threat of what she would write.

I made an offer for her to speak to my good friend who's an author, Wendy Dale. Wendy emailed and called her several times. Wendy knew why I stayed silent in 2019. She let me confide in her during the time I was getting death threats. She spent time on the phone calming my nerves, and even collaborated on a funny video about the Russian agent accusation, to try to bring me back to earth. Wendy had written a piece for Vox, so she reached out to Laura to share my story. Laura would not respond or read what she had to say, presumably because it did not fit with her narrative. The harm Laura caused me and other survivors with her article was long-lasting, and the ugliness of her ego was revealed by her omission of the truth.

At one point, I broke down sobbing while talking to Laura.

She said, "There, that is what I wanted."

She said it with glee, as if my crying made her satisfied and triumphant. In that moment, I felt weary about how truly awful and manipulative human beings could be to get their way.

I realized she was just a predatory reporter with an agenda. I did not know what the agenda was until the article appeared, and she refused to speak to my friend Wendy Dale, a professional writer, who has always stood by the fact that I never changed my story.

Laura had an angle and was relentless about it. I saw industry praise for her writing, but the other reporters had no idea about her key omissions and her lies.

As the movement to unseat Trump became more fervent, I suppose their rationale was that the sexual assault I had endured, and the loss of my career, were not as important as the Democrats needing to win the election. I was essentially the sacrificial lamb to the party. To them, the end justifies the means.

VOX HEADLINE: The agonizing story of Tara Reade - I started reporting on Tara Reade's story a year ago. Here's what I found, and where I'm stuck.

Unfortunately, things would get worse, including when *Washington Post* journalist Beth Reinhard reduced my corroborating witness to tears.

Rich McHugh entered my life in the middle of *the NYT* reporting. He was Ronan Farrow's reporting partner on the NBC scandals and the Harvey Weinstein case. He had seen powerful people throw around their status to silence survivors.

I called Rich the "gladiator for truth." I wasn't sure what his stance was or even if he believed me, only that he wanted the truth to come forward. Rich, like Ronan, are trauma-informed reporters. The way he asked me questions allowed me to relax and reveal details rather than shut down. Collin talked to him and seemed to be more satisfied with the neutrality. That is all any of us wanted, rather than the aggressive slants and politicization of the assault.

One morning at coffee, I received a call, "Tara?"

"Yes?"

"This is Ronan Farrow."

Ronan's voice was strong and unmistakable.

Finally, I thought, *there are reporters interested in getting to the heart of the matter, not just advancing their own agendas.* Like Rich, Ronan's approach was matter-of-fact but respectful. He, too, had trauma-informed reporting experience, and it showed in his manner and tone. The way he approached my situation was professional and cautious, sensing how caught up I was in the day-to-day news cycle drama of being a target for the media.

He would offer, "Tara, this is noise. Just noise."

Ronan would go on to speak to everyone I had told him about, but not working specifically on a piece about me. I became concerned that I would be his equalizer piece, and he would not believe me. Ronan had some remarkable talks with my daughter that gave her strength. I let go of the worry about being believed or not believed. Ronan was not interested in personalities either; he was interested in truth. The reporters to whom I had shared my most difficult experience were doing their jobs, unless they had a political motive.

I came to learn that if a reporter seemed neutral, it was a positive thing. During the late summer, *60 Minutes Australia* brought their camera crew to meet me in person and hear me out. The reporter, Alexis, had worked on many stories involving sexual misconduct and assault. She truly came from a trauma-informed space. I did not like the first promo they ran for the show, but it was soon replaced with a better one. The interview itself with *60 Minutes Australia* was very balanced and gave me a sense of dignity. The cameraman, Rich, was meticulous in his outdoor shots, and even let me inspect the drone camera. Instead of feeling nervous and on edge, I felt comfortable interacting with them and loved the richness of the Australian accent. The horses would not always cooperate with the shots, which led to laughter.

I learned about "the exclusive" from this experience. Reporters wanted to be the first to break the story and sometimes their competition was at the cost of the story. In my case, the interviews I gave with Megyn Kelly ruffled feathers. Chris Wallace had vied for one, but was very polite when I cancelled the night after the death threats. Don Lemon wanted me to come on CNN, even as the network stated outright lies about me. Don had sent a kind message saying sorry about the death threats that I had received. He even spoke directly with me on the phone. I almost went on his show, but finally chose to move forward with the Megyn Kelly interview. He sent me a text asking why I chose Megyn Kelly if I did not want to seem partisan?

Again, the assault was lost amongst the game of political football, with me as the football. Sean Hannity wanted an interview, but I was torn because my political home was in the liberal camp. I started to realize I no longer had a political home. But none of this stopped the negative media coverage, and the bullying online only intensified even after each positive interview that was conducted with someone in my life.

Anthony Zenkus called right after the third *NYT* article, "Tara, Lisa didn't seem interested in my expertise and perspective on sexual assault, trauma and domestic violence when we spoke on the phone. She actually spent a significant amount of time talking about how she'd been harassed and targeted on social media when those questions were released. She told me that she wasn't behind all of those questions and seemed to distance herself from them. I told her the questions represented rape culture–asking people things that have nothing to do with their sexual assault, such as, who you were dating, why you didn't leave your abuser right away, etc.

"She didn't seem interested. She spoke about how hard it was for her getting called out on Twitter, and I thought, *hey, you're not the victim here.* Didn't matter. When her article came out in *the NYT*, she dedicated one sentence to what I told her. 'Experts say...' It was a wasted opportunity to educate people about violence against women and others. And that article fed right into the rape culture narrative, along with *Politico* and the other articles. It didn't surprise me, but it just made me sad." Anthony was exasperated.

Even my supporters would get harassed relentlessly. Anthony had people attempting to get him fired. The brave journalists who first broke my story were harassed and harangued by trolls. It seemed I was causing problems for everyone, including my family. I wanted to disappear. There was no doubt I knew what had happened to me and the truth I presented, but with the social media trolls and mainstream media attacks, I started to feel like the monster they called me, and this further shook my confidence. I started to feel invisible again, because the essence of who I truly was as a person had been left out of the media's reporting. I was undone.

CHAPTER 4

Vlad

"We sit in mud and reach for the stars."
—Ivan Turgenev

I have not met Vladimir Putin. He was not president of Russia or even on the geopolitical horizon in 1993 when Joe Biden assaulted me. If the president of Russia bothers to follow American news media, he is probably wondering how he and Russia got dragged into a story that is solely about an assault Biden committed twenty-seven years ago.

I do not have an online Russian boyfriend or any boyfriend, husband, or lover, despite what *the NYT* writes in their hit pieces on me. That said, according to the social media trolls, I "have a Russian boyfriend who owns a Siberian horse farm," and that I will escape to this farm after the election. It sounds actually pretty nice because I do love horses. I'm not sure about Siberia. Maybe I should just let the trolls write the next chapter.

The Russia rumors started in 2019 when I was still writing my novel, which happened to be about Russia. Since I had never traveled to Russia, this took research and study. I was tired of seeing formulaic spy movies. Russia is always the villain in the films, and I wanted to explore the xenophobia by writing about the friendship between two girls, one Russian and one American. I was deep into my research and the outlines of a few chapters when the news broke. Immediately, I was dismissed as a Russian agent. I am not. Obviously. In 2020, I discussed *The Last Snow Tiger* and the Russia accusations against me on the podcasts *The Russian Guy* and *Primo Nutmeg*.

I have always been fascinated by the 1000-year-old Russian culture, history, and arts. I have a particular love for ballet and often listened to Russian composers while I was growing up. I also acted in an Anton Chekov's The Cherry Orchard." Chekov had good insight into human nature, much like American playwright Tennessee Williams. I grew up reading Tolstoy, Dostoevsky, Pushkin, and others. My mother almost named me Lara after Boris Pasternak's famous character from *Dr. Zhivago*.

One of my Russian friends still calls me Lara rather than Tara. I interviewed my Russian artist friend who lives in America about her views of President Putin. She is neutral and supports her government's education and health programs. She pointed out the gaps for any social help in America for its citizens. Overall, she is interested only in art, not politics. My friend Valentina is older and passionately supports her president. She discusses with me the scary '90s, food shortages, lack of infrastructure, and how hard life was before President Putin came into power. I asked some people in the area where Vera grew up about it. Several were neutral, but a couple of the younger men did not support President Putin. It was an interesting sample of views.

It was in 2019, after my story was published in the Grass Valley, CA newspaper The Union, that the internet trolling began. Within twenty-four hours, there was a conspiracy blaming the Russians, again.

A distant cousin called me, literally stuttering, "I just finished watching 'The Americans' and the tweets say you're illegal. A Russian agent?"

My head fell to the keyboard. "Ummm, what is that show? And I am related to you."

She laughed and asked, "I know, but you're writing… those blogs?"

"I am in a creative writing group, and I'm writing a novel. The poetry is for the novel and the blogs because I watch and read a lot of Noam Chomsky. I loathe xenophobia. I won't be told by power elites whom to like and what country to like. I love various cultures: Russian, Italian, and so many others."

She paused, pondered, and replied, "Hmmm, well this Norm Chomsky is a dissident, right?"

I sighed, "Its Noam."

"Yeah, right."

If we follow the strange logic that I was a Russian agent, or Soviet plant, or a "honeytrap," as I was called, would that somehow have made it okay for Biden to assault me?

I am a loyal American, and in the words of Lucy Flores, I was a "Democratic foot soldier." I voted despite all my troubles for the Obama-Biden ticket. Twice.

A friend who knew me back then and heard a pundit say, "Yes, well none of his former employees have come out," called.

My friend asked gently, "Tara, did you hear that?"

I sighed, yeah, the gauntlet had been thrown.

Later that day, a reporter called from *The Washington Post* after the allegations of being some sort of secret agent came out. "I read what was said about you in the *Daily Dot*. Edward Dovere implied you were a Soviet plant or spy. I mean he writes for *The Atlantic*" she added as if it must have made it true.

"I am not a Russian agent," I responded for about the twentieth time that day.

The red scare is alive and well in America. In fact, during one interview when I was feeling salty, a reporter asked me if I was a Russian agent.

"Nyet," I answered. "Nyet" means "no" in Russian.

My friend told me in a fierce whisper, "Don't speak Russian."

I guess it was too soon to make the joke. I rolled my eyes.

Oh, these Americans! The bloggers and writers cherry pick parts of my novel, to craft some sinister plot and indict me. But what they really do is change the conversation from Biden assaulting his junior staff member to how she is part of some obscure Russian plot-in-the-making…for twenty-seven years!

Once, I saw Joe Biden recount meeting Vladimir Putin. In Joe Biden's typical braggadocio, blowhard style, he said he was being shown around by the Russian president.

Biden allegedly said, "I looked into Vladimir Putin's eyes and saw no soul. I told him so."

He then went on to say, "Prime Minister, you have no soul."

According to Biden, Vladimir supposedly answered, "Now we understand each other."

I don't believe Joe Biden's version of the conversation, not for a minute. Joe Biden has been caught arrogantly lying many times, even about things he didn't need to lie about.

In 1993, I looked into Joe Biden's eyes. During my assault, his eyes were blank and soulless. Perhaps Joe Biden was projecting his own evil behavior onto someone else, when he made that comment about President Putin. It did make me wonder.

I wrote some blogs in 2019 about President Putin and Russia as I was doing a deep, creative dive into my novel. In that exploration of other cultures and views from world leaders, I tried to look through a lens other than the American neo-liberal lens that were my goggles for most of my life. I started reading other views. I watched Showtime's Oliver Stone interviews of President Putin, and I read Howard Zinn and Noam Chomsky. I am not ascribing my own views to Chomsky, Zinn, or Stone. They just presented a different view. I also read opposition to Russian leadership, including Julia Ioffe, Masha Greene, and others. In the Stone interviews, President Putin emphasized that he did not want war with our country, but rather that he wanted to advance peace. He also expressed that no matter what type of cooperation he extended, it was viewed suspiciously by his "American partners." He did express his frustration in a measured way during the interview regarding the anti-Russian propaganda coming from this country.

I got serious heat for even considering a different point of view and exploring the world with intellectual curiosity. My open-mindedness was conveniently used to invalidate what happened in 1993. The media didn't care about the gravity of calling someone a Russian agent. While it had become a joke among my family and friends, it increased the threats I received online.

For the last five years, the media has been hysterical with the Russian interference narrative. Its onset was a startling and constant barrage of negative stories on CNN. I tend to question when I am being force-fed an opinion, instead of being presented with objective facts in the news. If Russia and Putin have committed acts against humanity and worse, history will sort it out. This story, my story, is about a young American staffer who was sexually assaulted by her boss, an American U.S. Senator in the American Capital of Washington, D.C. It has nothing to do with Russia or Vladimir Putin. So, Russia, if you are listening, you are off the hook for this one.

#RoseTheOneWomanArmy

"America is the scariest cult I have ever been in."
—Rose McGowan

I am reminded I am not alone. There are angels that come into our lives; I was lucky enough to have a warrior archangel come into my life. Rose McGowan reached out to me at a time when facing each day had become excruciating. Rose saved my life.

At the same time the reporters circled me like vultures on political roadkill, there were other journalists who were simply intent on looking for truth, not politics. Some of these conversations brought light and healing. While I struggled to navigate everything daily, there were people who risked their professional credibility to hear and report my story. There were few public figures that even tiptoed around my allegations against Biden, with one notable exception.

Rose McGowan is a multimedia artist and former actor. She is a prolific creator of the arts. Rose starred in the docuseries "Citizen Rose" and directed the short film "Dawn," which was nominated for the Grand Jury Prize at the Sundance Film Festival. She also authored a book called Brave, directed an award-winning film, and produced and created a healing music CD called Planet Nine with healing theta beats. Rose also stood up against the Hollywood establishment by speaking her truth about Harvey Weinstein raping her. She stood up first and alone in her truth before the #MeToo movement, which led to other silence-breakers coming forward. Rose was and is her own movement.

One of the silence-breakers, a Harvey Weinstein survivor, reached out to me and asked, "May I give Rose McGowan your phone number?"

I replied, "Of course!"

Just a short time later, Rose called and asked in her distinct voice, "Hi, is this Tara Reade?"

I answered "Yes."

"This is Rose McGowan, and you are hard to find," she said with a chuckle.

"Yes, I am," knowing that it was true.

"I want you to know that I believe you," Rose said in a firm voice.

That simple and direct statement made me feel a rush of relief and gratitude.

Rose immediately put me at ease and shared her experiences with me, offering practical advice and even details of her journey that she had kept private. She gave me space to talk about what was happening and actively listened to my pain. Rose is one of the few public figures I have come to know who is exactly the same in public as she is in private. She has a fierce and refreshing authenticity that makes others want to reciprocate.

"I will tell you right now what is going to happen. They will come after you and your family," she warned quietly and sadly. "My life was almost destroyed by that monster (Harvey Weinstein). I was in handcuffs before my rapist was."

Rose had been arrested on trumped-up charges orchestrated by Harvey Weinstein and his spies. People posing as supporters, who were later identified as Mossad agents, had befriended her and infiltrated her life, trying to get information from her and about her book manuscript.

Ronan Farrow wrote in his book, *Catch and Kill* about the Israeli spies, and in his Pulitzer-Prize-winning reporting about the Weinstein case, he wrote about the mainstream media's pernicious effort to silence it. The podcast "Catch and Kill" featured his reporting partner, Rich McHugh, and their journey exposing the media and Harvey Weinstein's sexual predatory behavior. Rose and other survivors also discussed their journey on his podcast. I read about all this in the fall of 2019, after I had been called a Russian agent the prior spring. The book and podcast by Ronan Farrow helped me feel less isolated about my history with Joe Biden. It also gave me insight into the bizarre experiences I had while trying to come forward about Joe Biden in 1993 and again in 2019. My story never really picked up momentum, but rather, was simply spiked.

Rose's account of her experience shook me. Like her, I was getting online messages calling for me to be "locked up." These Democrats who trolled me mined for anything in my past that would help them make the case to incarcerate me. Would I be charged with some fabricated crime or somehow silenced? Months later, there would be accusations that I committed felony perjury as an expert witness, and an inquiry into possible prosecution began. Imagine coming out about a powerful person's crime and wondering if you could be arrested at any moment.

The Salem Witch Trials may have taken place in the 1600s, but our culture is still engaging in silencing and oppressing survivors who speak out. American institutionalized rape culture is alive and well. With the powerful and connected, nothing is off the table.

The torment Rose endured is the very reason survivors do not come forward about powerful men. Rose's courage gave me hope, solace, and resolve. Rose helped me in practical ways and also with emotional support.

At my lowest point, she gave me a strong push to stand up and not wither away. I needed it. She reminded me that everything I was going through she had already experienced, and more. This path she had forged was a rough one created by her trauma, blood, and tears, and I was next in line.

Every time I came under fire, Rose was present to fire back in my defense, even at the risk of her own career and personal relationships. Bill Maher came out attacking me in a blistering way in one of his show monologues. The next day Rose revealed her encounter with him and his own creepy misogynistic behavior. She called him out.

Alyssa Milano used her platform to galvanize votes for Biden. Her reaction to Christine Blasey Ford was strikingly different than her reaction to my allegations.

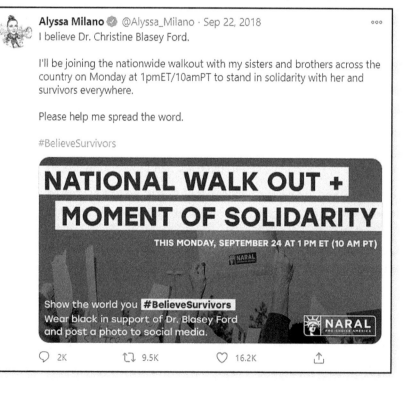

After a Twitter battle between Rose and Alyssa, I texted Rose a thank you for standing up for me. After Fox News and another print article covered the Twitter battle, Rose texted me wryly, "I do not think a *Charmed* reunion is happening anytime soon."

Later, Patricia Arquette would attack Rose on Twitter. I pushed a defense and Patricia fired back at me saying my story changed and began taunting

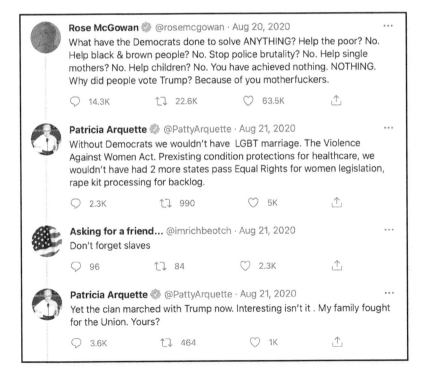

me.

The four of us engaged in a Twitter battle until we all ended up block-ing each other, part of it again ending up in the media. Rose defended me, and I defended Rose, while pointing out the hypocrisy of the Democratic Party.

During our conversations, she helped me navigate public relations and gave me sound advice and warnings. I listened, and I learned. Each tweet became a missive, crafted to advance my message.

Sadly, like many of my supporters, Rose experienced attacks from other professionals and even directly from her family, for supporting me. The Democratic vote-shaming with the talking points were repeated by all the neo-liberals.

The talks I had on the phone and via text with Rose McGowan made a very bleak part of my experience with media outlets bearable. In a world where kindness is rare, and at a time when social distancing is the norm, I felt close to something powerful and true. The shame and stigma of sexual assault had melt-ed away as Rose literally gave me strength to countere the avalanche of smears and harassment to come.

The other woman who stuck her neck out on the line for me is someone I have always had a low-key girl crush on. Megyn Kelly is powerful, intelligent, and independent. She is also an American journalist, attorney, and TV news anchor and host. She is who I want to be when I grow up, except she is a few years younger than me. My other female heroes, or "sheroes," are my mom, my daughter, my great grandmother Jane, Rose McGowan, Ethel Kenne-dy, Carole Lombard, Amelia Earhart, and Boudicca. Megyn Kelly is in esteemed company. I was surprised and pleased to get her direct message and then speak with her on the phone.

"How are you doing, lady?' Megyn asked.

"I am, well, it is hard." I said, trying not to sound flustered.

The day before her call, I had received a death threat and things were intense with the news media. I was cancelling my scheduled interview with Chris Wallace. He was gracious and forthcoming in every conversation, but after being up all night, and having to deal with law enforcement reporting the death threat, I did not feel poised for an interview.

Megyn and I talked for a while, and something about her just felt familiar. I was immediately at ease, not to mention a little star struck.

I asked, "You know, I was wondering if you would do the interview with me? I had wanted you to do the interview for a while."

Megyn paused, "Oh, well, thank you, but a platform?" I could tell she was thinking out loud.

"Do you know Rich McHugh?" I asked.

She answered, "Yes, I worked with him." She sounded enthusiastic at his name.

I said, "If he is willing, could you all do a piece?"

"Oh, yes, and let me look into it. I have an idea."

When we ended our call, I was hopeful she would at least consider it. I was not sure what would happen next, but I was not feeling ready for prime time. I just kept thinking about the death threats, my daughter being hounded, and threats that if I was not silent, there would be posts about my divorce, my bankruptcy, or more bottom-feeding trolls wanting attention or money. I felt bad about Chris Wallace. In every conversation, he was kind and open. However, moving on to the Megyn Kelly possibility was a risk. First, she may not have believed me. She was known to be a tough interviewer when taking on world leaders. How was I going to withstand that? But something told me it didn't matter if she believed me, I would just speak my truth and be direct.

The next time we talked, we discussed the logistics of the interview and timing. Megyn also asked if anything was off limits.

I said, "No. Nothing. You can ask me anything."

She was quiet and said slowly, "Okay."

After I hung up, I wondered if I should ask someone how to prepare, or if I should have questions that were off limits. In the end, I just let go and trusted the process, and my own ability to speak the truth.

I had gone on two other shows besides Katie Halper's show, sharing this difficult history, including *Rising with Krystal Ball* and *Democracy Now* with Amy Goodman. Krystal was direct, and the show was comfortable. Amy Goodman was another person I admired, and it was an amazing experience to be on her show. The hard part was the 3:30am call because of the live show. Also, you can't hear the rest of the show while waiting. You just get the cue that you're going on and voila, you are live.

This was going to be different. Rich McHugh was producing, and they were coming to me. At this time, I lived in the Grass Valley area of California, so we taped it at a Sacramento hotel. Megyn sent a car for my hair stylist and me. As I walked through the eerie lobby—emptied by Covid—to go to our suite, I started to feel butterflies. I was nervous to meet both Rich and Megyn in person. I had settled on a soft pink top because Megyn wore black. Rich, dressed in his east coast casual, looked tired and happy. He met me through a jungle of cords, and it was reassuring to see him.

Rich had written two investigative articles based on some really tough, but fair, questions. In all those conversations, he remained neutral about whether he believed my story. Like Ryan Grim and Megyn Kelly, for him, it was about the truth and not the personalities. I understood that, but sometimes I felt isolated talking to journalists during this time who were only sifting me like sand for truth. There was no real connection. Covid had put up a wall between me and normal activities, just like it had for everyone else, making it all the more challenging to come forward. That familiar loneliness enveloped me. I was walking into a strange moment of history.

Rich was warm and gracious as he greeted me. Megyn walked in and met me, shook my hand and put me at ease with a joke about how she was reading how much I liked Vladimir Putin. Megyn dressed in a simple black tank and shirt, charismatic and luminous. I laughed as she said, "One of my girlfriends likes him, and it's okay." She smiled mischievously. I didn't respond, because I confess I was still wary. I tried to banter back a bit, despite my uneasiness.

We sat as they adjusted for height, lighting, and framing. My stylist checked my makeup. One part of my bangs wanted to flop into one of my eyes, and I overcompensated by tilting my head to one side. Later, there would be body language experts examining my interview on YouTube and questioning this tilt of my head. This made me laugh, because it was just to prevent hair from falling in my face.

The lights felt warm in the air-conditioned room. I breathed deeply as Megyn asked if I was ready to begin. The room had been hushed while Rich was making computer adjustments. The lights and camera crew of two prepped quietly. Megyn looked at her notes while I sipped water. It started with Megyn asking me the first question. The forty or so minutes went by in a flash. I expected hard questions, but I also knew that I would have to give some tough answers.

I was thrown when she asked me about Putin, and tried not to act rattled. In my mind, it wasn't relevant; but to her it was. And it was because of the blogs I had written and the excerpts of the novel I was writing had been taken out of context. And I suppose her questions were to be expected. Megyn Kelly took a unique approach to the Russian question by cajoling me with a joke about my alleged crush on Putin. I didn't bite—on the record. Off the record, I gave her my view of the absurdity of the whole situation. It's true he's seen as a strongman. Perhaps in some subconscious way, I thought he was the only one who could take on Joe Biden. There has always been a part of me, for better or worse, that wanted to be saved from the situation with Biden, to witness some justice being rendered. However, I would have to come to terms with navigating my own way to justice and not rely on a man, real or fantasy, to save me. There was no knight in shining armor waiting in the wings. I had to go on my own hero's journey or live in denial. I did both. This was where my feminism and vulnerability met.

Rather than over-explaining anything in the interview, I gave short, honest answers. The hardest question was repeating what Biden said to me, and when she asked me what I was wearing. However, I answered each directly.

Megyn had provided everyone with a catered meal for lunch. She had thought of every detail. As I left the interview, I felt I had said all I wanted to say. I felt respected and relaxed. As we drove home, I had this feeling that someone had lifted a foot off my chest. It was a release of emotion, and the feeling was more profound than even my first real interview with Katie Halper.

Once home, I called my daughter and talked about Megyn Kelly.

"What was she like?" Michaela asked.

"She was just the same as when she was on air. Very funny and down to Earth."

"Did she seem like she knew it really happened or did she seem doubtful toward you?"

"She seemed like a journalist, but one that is trauma-informed. I mean she asked me tough questions and it was intense, but in a good way. It didn't feel like I was in a battle, like when I talk to other reporters."

"Well, I hope it's fair." Michaela responded, as she was now wary of journalists with agendas. I assured her Megyn was not like that.

"All I know is I feel better and relieved." I said with a sigh.

I tried to relax that night, but couldn't shake the tension. I listened to music to try to relax. I played Lorenna McKinnet's "The Mystic's Dream" and remembered my horse running on the beach when I was younger. In my mind, I was at a time when I was freer, before all of this had dragged me to a destiny and intensity I never wanted.

I drifted off as my cat lay in the curve of my arm, listening to the beat of hooves in my memory.

CHAPTER 6

The Art of Childhood

"We are such stuff as dreams are made of and our little life is rounded by a sleep."

—William Shakespeare

Recently, a video from *Larry King Live* dated August 11, 1993 resurfaced. In the video, a female caller questioned what her daughter should do after having experienced an unnamed 'issue' with a prominent Senator with whom she had worked. Looking to the show for advice, this mother knew her daughter was scared to go to authorities. We know now that her daughter had confided only in her mother, brother, and a few close friends about the extent of this unnamed issue. The mother did share that her daughter had been conflicted about speaking up -- out of respect for her employer, and that she wanted to succeed at her job.

Larry listened, as did his experts on the show.

The daughter with the issue was me. The Senator in question was Joe Biden, and the woman speaking in the video was my mother, Jeannette.

Hearing my mother's voice from so many years ago took my breath away. It was as if she were still alive.

My mother had piercing dark hazel eyes and stylish short black hair. She had high cheekbones and a very aquiline nose. She was beautiful in her youth and was unaware of her effect on men. She never had a chance to figure out what she wanted to explore in her life, because she was married and a mother by the age of sixteen. My mother loved the arts and instilled that love into all of us. My cousin, Janie, would always say how glamorous my mother was when she was younger and stylish.

Calling into *Larry King Live* was not the first time my mother stood up for me as it related to an abusive situation with a man. It's also not the first time where my mother's words fell on deaf ears. My mother's call being aired felt like time travel. Her voice across space and time validated that I had had a problem with Biden -- and that I told her about it. One headline read, "A Voice From the Grave." That is a mother's love - timeless and powerful.

Like any human being, my mother was imperfect -- especially when it came to her drinking. But despite her flaws, I knew two things about her with certainty.

One: my mother loved me with all her heart.

Two: my mother definitely knew an abusive man.

My childhood had many idyllic moments, but there were challenges, too. My fondest memories are from living on the farm and connecting with those eighty acres of nature. I would get up early and be out until dark, playing with my pony, Bullitt, in the pasture or in the barn. I would climb up to the top of the hay bales and swing down. I loved the sweet smell of dried alfalfa and the safe pace of the upper barn. There were barn cats and often kittens to cuddle amid the bales of hay. I would bring my books and read. When I was hungry, I would dig through my mom's garden or grab a Popsicle. I was skinny and tall, with hair down past my shoulders, and always running.

My father loved the farm, but worked in town running his advertising agency, which left all the labor to my mother -- which she didn't like. It left her feeling isolated with two small children.

She delved into her one-acre garden and her art for escape. My mother canned, so mostly everything we ate was from the farm. I remember following her into the garden and kneeling with her as we plunged our hands into the soil. I would watch when she sat at her vanity to put on makeup and Chanel No. 5.

"You are my little shadow," she would say, giving me a smile and a beep on the nose.

Conversely, I tried to stay out of my father's way. He was a large man;

people described him as a big bear. He had black hair and ice cold blue eyes. He laughed robustly, and his humor engaged people, even when his temper surprised them.

There was a time -- before I dreaded my father -- when I loved him. However, I don't remember it well. Our problems began when I was very young.

He hurt me physically and emotionally many times, but perhaps one of the most painful was when he killed my dog Boo. I had heard stories about times he used to take my mom's little dog Pixie Sue and put her on the hood of the car, then drive slowly while she shook, terrified. There were times he would bite Pixie Sue's ear until she yelped.

My little Boo was a scruffy small terrier mix. He liked to bark, which annoyed my father. Boo really liked to trail my bigger dog up the driveway, to greet the car whenever we got home from somewhere. One day as we drove in, both dogs greeted us running. On one occasion, I was in the backseat when my father's eyes met mine in the rearview mirror. He swerved the car suddenly and we heard Boo yelp. I immediately started screaming; so did my mother. My father was silent as he went looking for the little dog, who was howling in pain. My mother would not let me follow him, so she took me into the house—and that's when we heard the gunshot.

My mother came into my room later with a tray of soup, as I lay curled up sobbing. She soothed me with a washcloth and said, "Tara, Boo had internal injuries so your father had to shoot him. He feels terrible. Go out and say good night."

I shook my head no.

She explained, "Your father would never do that on purpose."

I didn't respond. Nor did I tell her about him making eye contact with me in the mirror. I just cried, wanting to disappear.

Later, to cope, I would imagine Boo's spirit was running joyfully alongside my dog Clown and me. It was not the first time my father would break my heart with his cruelty and it would certainly not be the last. I briefly lived with my father when I was fourteen, and was removed by Child Protection Services (CPS) because he was extremely physically abusive. I still remember the CPS worker, Richard Spratt.

He said, "I am going to save you years of therapy, Tara. Go back to your mom's house. Sometimes parents do not love their children. Your father does not love you. Go live with the parent who loves and wants you."

Excellent advice. I barely spoke to my father again until I graduated from high school. Mind you, he didn't show up at my graduation. My mother gave me flowers, new clothes and a cake. Even as her addiction to vodka intensified, and our mother-daughter battles became more frequent during my teens, she always showed me love. I knew her love was unwavering, yet there were still times I pushed it away.

My mother became an artist and activist. She grew up in a small California town called Avenal. Her mother and father, my grandparents, were devoted to each other. My mother was the youngest of four children. My grandfather was someone I never met, but whom my mother adored. My mother called him Daddy whenever she spoke of him. I found it unusual that she called him Daddy because I would never call *my* father that.

She would sigh, pat my head and apologize, "I am sorry, Tara, that I didn't have better for you. You deserve a father who loves you. I know I was lucky. "

I nodded and felt that empty gnawing. I knew it was a void that I could never fill.

My father never loved me and often told me that growing up. When I was thirteen, he declared in court that I was illegitimate just to avoid child support. My mother came home that day and hurriedly opened the freezer to her vodka.

"Your father says you are a bastard, Tara. Just remember that he is the bastard, not you," she shared while plunking ice in her drink.

I went into my room and lay on my bed looking at the ceiling. I spent the next hours listening to my Eagles album and drawing sketches. *I don't care,* I told myself, but hot tears ran down my face because everyone thought I was a bastard.

I wondered about the court hearing and how many people heard. Would everyone know? I had not heard that term a lot, but I knew what it meant: that he was not my father. I was glad. I thought, *who would want him as a father anyway*? I still felt sick and sad. My dog wandered in, hopped on my bed, and stayed with me while I cried until I fell asleep.

My mother told me the story about how her father had died of a sudden heart attack a month or so after he retired. He had worked in the oil fields all his life and supported much of the extended family during the depression. He got a gold watch and some stock at retirement. My uncles were wildcatters who won and lost fortunes during the California oil boom.

My mother wanted nothing more than to leave the desert town of Avenal, and she did. She married and went to live in Saudi Arabia, Libya, England and Malta. But my mom fell in love while in Malta. I'd seen the pictures of my mother during that time. She looked glamorous and adventuresome.

Her first husband was absent a lot and, at times, brutal to my mom. She had known a different upbringing and did not accept the mistreatment at the time.

One night, my mom and I were drinking sparkling wine and she giggled.

I asked, "What, Mom?"

Mom played with the stem of her crystal wine glass, "Oh, I was just thinking of Joe Scicluna, how he brought champagne the night he serenaded me." Mom sighed slowly.

"He did know how to romance a girl," she laughed. "He used to call me his enigma." Mom waved her hand. "Little did he know I adored him, but back then we did not let on."

Into our second glass of wine, she started talking more. She sat curled in her blue, silky gown, her feet tucked, and waving her hands, one of which had a beautiful freshwater pearl ring on it, as she described the gorgeous estate in Malta and her life there. The Marquis Joe (also an artist) was the great love of her life. Mom had lived with Joe for a couple of years, and they had a passionate affair while she separated and divorced from her first husband. Their relationship ended tragically, because she was unable to leave her two children from her first marriage, my two older half-brothers. And his parents disapproved of a divorcee (which was a rare thing at the time.)

Joe and my mother exchanged letters even after they ended until he died. He never married. My mother sent flowers to his grave.

Joe had estates in Italy, England, and the Dragonara on the island of Malta.

Dragonara is now a gambling casino and a public place. At the time my mother was there, in the early 1960s, she stayed with Joe at the estate among his beautiful mosaics. Those are the same mosaics he hid in the famous catacombs where, as a child, he bunkered up during the WWII bombings. The Marquis was an accomplished artist and part of the Knights of Malta.

My mom described him as flamboyant and expressive with an eccentric streak. He and my mother did art together, listened to opera, and loved each other with an intense passion.

"Joe was so Italian in his manner. He was Italian and Maltese. He was always giving me flowers and gifts. He would say, 'Madam,'" mother then deepened her voice and imitated his accent, "'are you free to join me for dinner this evening?'"

Mom giggled, and her face worn from the years and puffy with alcohol, seemed younger and more vibrant for a moment.

"We would go to those fancy affairs where they announced you and your title. I met Gadhafi at one of those. He was young and so handsome and charismatic." Mom waved her hand. "Of course, this is before he came to power; too bad he turned into a tyrant. Sadly, Americans do not understand the Middle East. We are so young in our politics and views."

We sipped our drinks quietly, my mother lost in her thoughts and memories. I waited patiently. I fingered the cross and medallion necklace of Saint Cecilia that Joe had given mom to give to me. I wore it often.

My father, Robert, never liked to hear about the Marquis during his thirteen-year marriage to my mom. He would rage with jealousy at even a mention of Malta. It was a sore point, as I think he subconsciously knew he did not have the special place in my mother's heart that Joe did. When they divorced, I was twelve years-old and had witnessed years of drunken rampages they unleashed. My father was unfaithful to my mother from almost the beginning, and he would be cruel to her about it.

I was born in Monterey, California soon after my mother had returned to the states and met my father. My father was in a local play, and my mother was painting the scenery. It wasn't love at first sight. My mother said they met at a cast party and my father told her there was something ugly about her personality -- but that he found her fascinating. My mom returned the insult. I imagined it was like watching Elizabeth Taylor and Richard Burton's drunken insults in the *Lost Weekend* whenever my mother described their courtship.

My father left his two children with his first wife and went off with my mother. They lived in Pacific Grove, CA with a roommate. Their front door didn't work, so everyone climbed through their bedroom window. No one knew a locksmith, I guess. My parents were pre-hippies, or beatniks, and would write poetry for their dinner. My mother painted the restaurant sign design for Doc's Place on Cannery Row. My father would give up his Hemingway phase to write a sports column in Wisconsin, and opened his own advertising agency.

A few months after my birth, my mother, my older brothers, Michael and Brent, my father, and I packed up and headed to the north woods of Wisconsin. My brother Collin was born later.

My parents were both classic extroverts and were always surrounded by people. They were popular with their friends in Wausau, and could serve the best martinis in town at their dinner parties. The young professionals, and of course the artists, were their scene. My mother founded the Art in the Park in Wausau and won awards for her art. They both had their style and charisma. My mother was outspoken and my father sarcastic and funny.

People always wanted to please my father, including grown men and, of course, all his children, but no one could ever please him. His entitled arrogance was taken as confidence. My parents and their friends were loud and lived hard. My father could be cruel, and he liked to watch the hurt he caused. I learned this as I experienced his cruelty as a child; he would like my tears and defeat. If I was successful at anything, he would berate me and tell me I was shit. He loved to steal people's self-confidence. Like most bullies, he was indignant if anyone fought back.

"Charlie (his nickname for my mother), let me see your nails. Good god, how ugly."

He would take the hand of the woman that was visiting, "See Charlie, that is how a woman's hands should look."

He would hold up the other woman's hand in my mom's face. My mother would sometimes scream back at him or go in her room and cry when he would humiliate her in public.

My mother also gardened, and worked hard on the house. Her nails reflected someone who was busy painting, working with clay, cleaning, and not sitting around minding her perfect polish.

My father put her down a lot, calling her names and shoving her. I watched this as a small child, taking in the storms that made up my parents' relationship.

Mom was considered a "radical," and even on a watch list with the authorities due to her vocal protests of the Vietnam War. Michael, one of my older brothers by over a decade, joined the Army before his number was called, and was a conscientious objector. He even spent time in a Buddhist monastery. Michael died young after returning from overseas. I never knew the full scope of his experiences, only that he was forever changed and unalterably saddened by what he saw.

At one point, my mother was a member of the Committee Against Racism in Madison, Wisconsin. After the passing of my mother, I looked for the letter from the Wausau Public Library asking my mother to stop holding meetings about sending men to Canada to dodge the draft. The letter was polite, asking my mother to please stop meetings, to discuss what amounted to treason against the United States government, at the public library. Collin and I laughed at the polite plea in the letter, composed in that ever-folksy Wisconsin tone.

I was raised going to marches as a child and a tween in Chicago, with my mom. Houston Stevens, a Chicago organizer, would set up accommodations for us on the Southside of Chicago as we went door-to-door and attended marches for social causes, with Leftists.

The city of Chicago seemed huge to me as a child. In Wisconsin, living on our farm, it was a half-mile to a neighbor and twenty miles to the nearest town.

Chicago was a mythical beast of a city and a somewhat magical place in my imagination. On my transistor radio, I would pick up Chicago radio stations of jazz and talk stations, imagining the people and huge buildings. In person, Chicago seemed to smell of wet concrete, metal and fuel. The gatherings we attended were diverse and cozy. There were amazing food potlucks, and the adults smoked weed and drank wine while pontificating about their theories to create a better world for us. I ran and played with the other children on the brick-enclosed courtyards protected by idealism.

My father never attended or supported these political activities. He went politically where it suited his pocket book. After my parents' divorce, my father had top security clearance at the Pentagon and worked with defense contracts. As a young adult, I confronted him and accused him of selling "bombs and bullets." After that argument, we did not speak for years. That was the cover for a deeper chasm that existed between my father and all his children, but especially me.

As a small child I would look at the stars. In the deepest heat of summer, I would sneak out to the pasture with a blanket and mosquito spray to watch the night sky. I loved the fireflies and imagined them to be fairies with secret messages. The horses would be quietly grazing nearby. We lived so far from any city that the Milky Way was immense and it seemed as if you could grab the stars. Sometimes in fall, you could see the Aurora Borealis multi-color display when you looked north toward Canada.

I loved these quiet nights of listening to frogs and watching the fireflies until the mosquitoes became unbearable, even with the spray. I loved this solitude, as our house was always filled with visitors and their children on weekends. My parents found that surrounding themselves with people and music kept their scenes with each other at bay. That is, until it didn't. I was an introvert-extrovert and did not discover this until I was much older. It means that I found all the people going in and out overwhelming at times, even though I appeared outgoing. I have always found speaking to a group or performing in a play easier than speaking to smaller groups. I tend to keep to myself and need lots of alone time.

My parents' alcohol-fueled weekend-long parties were exhausting to me at times. I remember getting Collin, who was just a baby at the time, from his room when I heard him crying, scared by all the adults. I would fix him a bottle and take him to my bedroom to read to him or just to go back to sleep.

My mother's art was beautiful. She worked in watercolors, oils and sculptures. She always had a work in progress. However, she also lived up to the stereotypical artist temperament. My mother was brilliant, creative, and when she drank her vodka, she drank a great deal of it. The marriage to my father was her undoing. She tried to commit suicide twice during my life. I would later learn about the specifics of the first time she tried. It was during my mother's distraught state after walking in on my father with another woman (my mother's best friend) in bed.

This particular summer afternoon there was a muggy stillness. I lay next to the fan in my room, reading with my cat and dog curled next to me. Collin played with his Legos on the floor. My friend Anya was out with her parents on errands, and due to come by later for a sleepover, and she planned to bring her telescope. My mother had been crying in the morning. When I asked her why, she shooed me out of her room. It left me with a dull anxious feeling that gnawed at me. I was ten years-old and had some understanding of the seriousness of her tears.

Michael was playing his recorder. I could hear the soft Korean flute melody from my room. I heard a sharp bang, then running, and the breezeway door slam, then more running. I sat up, then lay back down, too hot to move. Something was definitely wrong. I quietly got up and walked out to see my brother Michael waving his hands and yelling something.

I moved closer to see my mother sitting in the field sobbing, "BOB."

She screamed, "You Bastard!!"

I could hear snatches of her words, screaming and then muffled intensity, "Bastard," "Kill," "Die," "WHY, oh god, why are you doing this?" More screams and other words, some I did not know. She had the barrel of the gun pointed at her temple, sobbing and screaming her rage. I could only catch bits of what she was saying. I felt cold and frightened, not quite comprehending what I was seeing, and then I heard myself scream.

My father came out of the barn entrance and stood, distant, like a silent crow, watching my mother, but did nothing. Michael grabbed the gun from my mother's hands and threw it far into the field. My father turned away and returned to the barn. My mother lay sobbing as Michael bent down holding her shoulders and rocking her like a small child. I felt frozen and tasted metal in my mouth as if I felt the barrel of that gun against my own tongue. I turned and ran inside. Collin was still playing on my floor. I went out back and got my red Radio Flyer wagon. I then got a suitcase and started packing my clothes and favorite stuffed animals. I went over to my record player. Realistically, I could fit only my brother or the record player and my music in the wagon. I pondered the choice and decided to take Collin. Collin laughingly climbed into the wagon with one of his Legos, saying, "Tata, let's go for a ride," in his toddler vernacular. I pulled the wagon with one hand, and slung a backpack over my other shoulder. We started down the long driveway away from the house. Michael caught up to me.

"Hey, Tara, where are you and Collin going?" he asked in his soft, kind voice.

"We are leaving here, Mikie. I can't stay here anymore. Collin wants to go too. You can come if you want."

"I would miss you and Collin so much if you left. How about I fix you some sandwiches and ice tea? Then we can make some homemade raspberry ice cream. What do you think?"

I rolled my eyes and said, "I am not pretending that nothing is wrong. I saw the gun and…"

Suddenly, I was overcome with tears, as Michael held me and said, "You must have been so scared to see that, darling. I am so sorry."

I was still crying as we stopped in the yard near the pond. He took the blanket and spread it out in the shade for Collin to play and for me to sit and rest. The wagon was heavy, my heart felt sick, and the heat wore me out. Michael sang the song he would sing to me to put me down for naps when I was five…rubbing my forehead. The song, Jean, from the musical *Oliver*. My eyelids felt heavy as he sang the song, "*Run if you will, to the top of the hill…*" and I fell asleep under the big maple tree.

When I woke up, I panicked and asked where mom was. Michael shushed me and reassured me she was resting in her room. All was okay again. Collin was asleep, too, and he carried him into the house while I dragged behind with the wagon. After going into the house, I rinsed off in the bathroom to wake up while Michael quietly made food for us.

Michael had a way of slowing down even the most frenetic day. He was always my protector and security. When he died a few years later, my life would never feel that warm or secure again. I searched for that unconditional love in work, in men and even in myself. The feeling of home evaporated into the heavens and left me utterly alone. I adapted, but never truly adjusted to his absence.

On this particular day, Michael's Buddha-like calm helped me. I still felt uneasy, but not that unhinged panic.

I went in to peek at my mom as she slept. She looked so pretty in her sundress with little lace bric-a-brac daisies at the border. I went out to the garden and picked her flowers. Then I made a card with glitter to tell her how much I loved her. I put it next to her bed. Maybe she wouldn't go away if she knew how much we loved her.

Later, Michael, Collin and I were eating, and my mother walked in to make coffee. She came over to me and enveloped me in a perfumed hug, thanking me for my flowers. She kissed my head over and over in almost a desperate way. She went and played her music - Peggy Lee's "Black Coffee" and some other jazz. The summer storm was over, for now.

But the storms would continue throughout my life. My mother loved to read different classics and modern writers. One year for my birthday, she gave me a book of poetry by Merrit Malloy, the Irish American poet, *My Song for Him who Never Sang for Me*. The last gift she gave me on my birthday before she died were two more of her books, one by Rod McKuen and one by Erica Jong. My mother loved Erica's raucous sense of humor and direct style of writing. When I would bring her one of my poems, she would nod and say, "This is a good start. Now, remember, show don't tell the reader. Let the reader come to you. You got it."

I took her advice to heart. She would laughingly tell that story of how when she was a "beatnik," as they were called at the time, she and my father would write poetry for free dinners at a restaurant in Cannery Row in Monterey.

The night of my assault with Senator Joe Biden, I called my mother and told her about it right away. I cancelled a date with my new boyfriend, who would later become my husband. I also wasted no time telling Collin and my friend Maeve.

I told them how I had been asked to deliver a duffle bag to the Senator, how he stopped me in the corridor and sexually assaulted me by putting his hands under my clothing and violating me. My story was corroborated in *The NYT*s by a friend of mine, and by my brother in *The Washington Post*.

My mother, whom I miss so much, especially now, knew everything.

What Is a Youth?

"What is a youth, impetuous fire, what is a maid, ice and desire the world wags on. A rose will bloom, it then will fade, so does a youth, so does the fairest maid."

—What Is a Youth, Zeffirelli's & Rota's Romeo and Juliet song, 1968

"The worlds a stage and we are merely players."

—Shakespeare

When I was young, my father acted in and directed community theatre. The first play I remember watching was *Camelot*. I memorized all the songs and some lines. In Romeo and Juliet, I loved to play the part of Tybalt and Mercutio, acting out the sword fights and pretending I was riding a horse.

My favorite toy was my record player. I spent hours dancing to Swan Lake and listening to the audio version of Zeffirelli's *Romeo and Juliet*. My older brother, Michael, and my mother read me poetry and Shakespeare. At five-years-old, I would recite Shakespeare to audiences in the break room at the community theatre. Michael loved my singing, and I would sing him the theme to *Romeo and Juliet*. Years later, when he died, I sang it as we spread his ashes over the Pacific Ocean. I always remember understanding the old English prose, and my love for theatre developed.

For my entire childhood and part of my early adulthood, I dreamed of being an actress and poet. My first play was Princess and the Pea. I played the Princess, and my brother Michael joked that I invoked the 'method' style when I started complaining about my back around the house, and suddenly wanted a new bed. My mother called me Desdemona, rolled her eyes, and said I was not getting a new mattress. I started getting more lead roles in junior high and high school. I went to several schools as my parents moved around after the divorce, but I stayed keen in my interest with the theatre. In high school, I had a group of drama geek friends whom I loved. Laura was blonde and I was brunette, so we got parts that were good fits for each of us, and where we both benefited. My friend Ilene had a beautiful mane of red hair and was a very good actor as well. Our Athens, Georgia high school was enthusiastic about football and the plays we put on. We had pretty good attendance to our plays, and we went to State First Act Plays Competition Trials with our one act plays.

I played Rizzo in *Grease*, and my first boyfriend played opposite me. Cal was a theatre geek like me and also into music. He was always creative. He was a wonderful first boyfriend and we have remained friends our whole lives. In fact, my friend Laura (who stayed in theatre and went on to perform Shakespeare in the Park in New York City and Prague) messaged me recently on Facebook.

"Tara," she said when we talked, "Cal is sticking up for you with all that negative press. Cal even got a call from *The NYT*."

My high school friends stood ready to help, and supported me even though they were mostly Democrats. I stayed in touch with them privately, on and off through the years. Social media has had many faults, but it was good to connect with some of the good friends I had from my youth.

My mom worked for public television in Athens while I was in high school. She had many neighborhood and work friends in our small cul-de-sac house. My mom was a huge football fan and loved the Georgia Bulldogs. She would prepare snacks, and the whole neighborhood would come over to our house with chairs, to follow the games on every TV and radio. Herschel Walker had burst on the scene as a young athlete. He and Buck Belue dominated every team. I would sit up on the hill with high school friends, and we would have our party watching the game. I saw Herschel leap over a pile of people and run a touchdown. Even at sixteen years old, I was in awe of his talent. My teams were Georgia Bulldog for college and Green Bay Packers for the NFL.

I distinctly remember the time Herschel Walker caused a local media stir when he and Buck Belue, the quarterback, walked in together at a traditionally 'white' bar together. My mother, who had been involved with the committee against racism for years, noted to Collin and me how brave that was of Herschel because of how dangerous it could be for black men, even football heros.

My eldest brother Brent had remained in Wisconsin with his wife Kathy. Brent was always supportive of whatever Collin and I were doing. Later, as I began work on TV and film with walk-on parts, he recorded some of my roles on *Highway to Heaven* and the dancing role in *La Bamba*.

At sixteen, I booked my first paid modeling gig for a print catalog. I would continue to follow my dreams to California. In Santa Barbara, I was once at the estate of esteemed Academy nominated actress Dame Judith Anderson. I had just starred in a local theatre production.

I did two contrasting monologues, including one from Shakespeare. I stood in a beautiful arboretum overlooking her estate gardens, while Anderson sat in the front row with a walking stick, watching. I could smell the sea air as I took my mark on the stage. I wanted to experiment with my scene, so I broke the third wall for part of my monologue. After I presented my pieces, I heard clapping and then, Dame Judith tapped her walking stick on the floor twice for silence.

Much to my mortification, she said, "Young lady, you have presence and proper elocution, but never ever (said with English emphasis) break the third wall."

She nodded to complete her point and silence came from the afternoon audience. I felt a flush. I was a bit ahead of myself and my time, breaking the third wall in a part of the play that did not call for it.

Acting was my artistic expression and release. I could bury myself in someone else's life for a little while. I loved the feel of the stage and butterflies fluttering in my stomach right before the curtain rose. I accepted any role I could and auditioned frequently. One of the most exciting auditions was for the Juilliard School of Drama. Their selection process is rigorous; after thousands of auditions, only twenty-two people are chosen to join the company.

I rehearsed for months and polished my iambic pentameter (rhythm of Shakespeare prose.) I met with Robert Reed several times right before he became ill and died. Robert was generous, kind, and worked hard with me to develop my monologues. His family mansion in Pasadena was exquisite, with sculptures and paintings from the masters. We practiced in a sitting room with a huge old fireplace that set the mood for my Shakespearean piece. At this point, I was working on subtlety and technical presentation. Robert Reed was a classically trained actor. I did not ask him about *The Brady Bunch*, but rather his stage roles. He loved my lasagna. I brought it as a gift once and then promised it again. Tragically, he died before I could bring it to him.

After a ton of hard work, I was selected for the semi-final audition for Julliard and flew to New York City. I practiced and then spent some free time walking around parts of Manhattan, smelling the cocktail of pavement, mixed with food, and steam rising from the sidewalks. Exhaust fumes, shouting, and lights bombarded my senses as I adjusted to the bustle of the big city. I walked to a small café in Little Italy to have a cup of coffee.

The owner, who was probably in his seventies, pulled up in a town car. His girlfriend, probably in her forties, had highly coiffed bright red hair. They were dressed impeccably. I was drinking espresso and reading a paper quietly, when I heard a question about me being asked in Italian. I looked up and answered my name in Italian. He walked over and thanked me for coming in and asked me how I was doing. I told him I was from California and auditioning for Juilliard. He shouted 'Brava," and took my hands raising them in the air in celebration. Everyone laughed.

He continued talking to me and said I could walk anywhere near these streets and no one would bother me. I thanked him. He gave me a free cannoli and told me to come back after the audition. He lamented that the neighborhood had changed and all his friends had moved to Long Island. The friendly welcome to New York City from this man helped put me at ease as I prepped for my audition.

Waiting for your number to be called is nerve wracking when at an audition. I sat in the Julliard waiting area and got to know one of the other women also auditioning. We went to dinner afterward and chatted about how we thought our auditions went. We were both called back the next day.

This was it, I thought, *my opportunity*. This was the moment I had waited, worked, and hoped for. My audition went well; I almost felt disassociated. I was so happy. One of the instructors sitting at the table spoke to me privately. She asked if I could afford tuition and housing (Juilliard is at Lincoln Center, so off-campus student housing was required.) I stammered my answer, "Yes, no... I am not sure. Are there scholarships?"

She pursed her lips thoughtfully, "I am sorry, not until your junior year is that kind of aid available."

I had not spoken to my father that year after he was a no-show for my high school play and graduation. However, I needed to figure something out in order to attend Juilliard, so I drew up my courage to call him.

At this time, my father wrote about and worked in the defense and aerospace industry that had made him very successful financially. Neither of my mother's jobs in graphics and design work -- the one at public television or at Cal Poly in California -- was lucrative enough to pay my way.

"This is Bob Moulton." He always answered the phone in this firm voice.

"Hi, Dad?"

"Who is this?" He knew very well who it was but wanted me to grovel.

"Dad, this is Tara. I'm in New York City. I landed an audition to get into the Juilliard School," I said this all in one breath.

Complete silence from him.

"So, umm, well, there is tuition and I do not qualify for aid because of your income." I was stating the obvious. He also had more money from not having to pay child support since I was now over eighteen.

"That's not my problem. Call your Congressman," he answered sarcastically.

"Dad, this is a once-in-a-lifetime opportunity, and I would be guaranteed work afterward or some real placement at least. I could pay you back," I pleaded.

"No, do something practical with your life. Go to law school. You argue well."

"Dad, please. This is, please, I worked hard to get this far, please." I was begging and now in tears.

I continued my plea, "I have a car. I could give you the title to the car." Unfortunately, my car was an old Delta '88 Oldsmobile, probably worth less than $500.

"Tara, I said, 'No.'" Then he hung up.

I stood staring at the pavement, hyperventilating until I was dizzy with grief. I flew back to California the next day.

On the way home from the airport, my Delta '88 got two flat tires. I sobbed at the side of the road.

My brother Michael came to get me. He was in remission from cancer and on his way to becoming a writer at the time. Michael always made me feel like I could do anything. It was not the first time he picked me up after my father pulled some horrible stunt based on what I wanted.

Before I had started college, my father offered to help me for the first time. But he created a rule: that I could not do any acting jobs. He found out about a play in Carpentaria I was in, because it was in the paper. And at that, he pulled his support. Michael had made me feel better then too.

"Some kids rebel by self-destructive behavior, like drugs. And your rebellion is to do theatre and you are successful. I will never understand Bob Moulton. He is such a cold bastard," Michael said about our father.

Michael rarely ever said anything mean or unkind about anyone. He was a Buddhist and believed in no harm. However, he and my father never got along. Michael, my half-brother thirteen years older than me, protected me and adored me. He was quiet and mild mannered, but my father would taunt him relentlessly. My father once broke Michael's jaw in an argument. My other older half-brother, Brent, was better at dealing with dad than Michael and knew how to avoid him.

My father and I would have years, even a decade or two, of not speaking. Our estrangement ended when he was very close to death. It was late, but when the call came from the nurse in Los Angeles, I spoke with him. He apologized to me for, in his words, "being a terrible father."

My father had a family before ours and abandoned two girls. We never really knew each other and met only once we were adults. One of them was at his bedside. He was otherwise alone.

The nurse said he was agitated, so I talked about sailing. My father loved to sail and even sailed to Cuba with a friend once. I let him go with love.

Two days later, a beautiful male pheasant landed in my backyard. All the neighbors were wondering where a pheasant came from, which was not at all common in the coastal area where we lived. I watched it wander in the yard and hop out at night. My father was always well dressed and dapper. I like to think it was his way of waving goodbye to me, as he departed on his journey.

The many hurts and pain I endured slipped away slowly over the next couple of years after I learned to forgive my father. However, at nineteen, I was still devastated by his abrupt call not to support my attendance to Juilliard.

The year during which I was still grieving over Juilliard, I met one of the loves of my life, Fabian. He was from Argentina and grew up in Los Angeles. He was half Italian and half Argentinian. Fábe was funny, kind, and handsome. I loved him deeply, and we lived together for a few years. Once, he flew me to London as a surprise and asked me to marry him at St. Pauls' Cathedral. It was beautiful and romantic.

One of the big differences we had is that I was not into partying and he was still going through that phase. It would lead to some hard times for him later. For several reasons, we never married, but always remained friends. My trajectory took me a different direction.

Some of my happiest memories were of the adventures we had together in our twenties and our friends. I used to ride my horse, do my theater, and audition. Fábe would drive me to certain auditions and gigs and looked out for my safety. Fábe was the best boyfriend in many ways. He had a compassion that he was never afraid to express. I understand he is now happily married with children, and has been sober for many years.

My time in Hollywood was exciting and interesting. I met famous directors, attended awards shows and had small walk-on parts. I landed an agent named Jack Scagnetti. He was wizened by Hollywood and New York. He looked at my résumé.

"What's all this Shakespeare shit? Shakespeare's out," he declared.

I could literally imagine the Bard's spirit aghast as he heard this being said by some showbiz guy in North Hollywood.

Jack looked me up and down slowly and clinically. I was five feet and nine-and-a-half inches and 125 pounds.

"You got great tits," He said. "I can get you some topless work."

I sighed and left his office. I was not interested in topless work, so I went to search for another agent. I auditioned for plays and landed roles. I took acting classes and went to a community college.

During these years, I decided to go backpacking in Europe for several months, alone, and had the trip of a lifetime. Although, one time when I was in

Italy, guard dogs that had been abandoned near a monastery once attacked me.

I had just had a wonderful lunch of fresh pesto, pasta, and home-made rolls, and some sparkling water. It was siesta time when all stores closed, but I was restless and took a walk. I felt a push on my back. I grabbed my money belt with one hand, thinking I was being robbed, but as I turned my head, all I saw were big, sharp canine teeth and heard low growls. I screamed, kicking and fighting, as I scrambled myself together I began running. The two dogs chased me to the ravine and I dove down and made it up to the road. The dogs stood vigilant at the edge of the meadow. One had my bloody sandal in her mouth. Cars were speeding around the curve, then a nice Jaguar pulled over. I was in shock and stood there.

"Adaiamo," he said. "Hospitale?"

I looked at my torn dress, and my leg and arm were covered in blood from the bites. I could see the ligaments of my leg, got woozy, and dropped to my knees. The Good Samaritan scooped me into his car and drove me to the hospital in Verona, no one spoke English. I speak a small amount of Italian but not medical terms. They used my American Express card interpretation services to call my mother. I am anesthesia-sensitive, which I learned about when I was having my tonsils removed, and my heart stopped. After getting this information from my mother, the doctors decide not to use any anesthesia. My leg and arm required stitches. They strapped me down, and, in Italian, told me to count...in Italian. When I could no longer take the pain, I was to say, "Basta" (enough).

They would count, and I tried to make it to at least twelve (docdici), so their repair of my leg and arm could go faster. I felt the stinging, burning pain and aches as they worked. A male nurse kept rubbing my head with a cloth saying, "pourvo bambina" (poor baby). Afterwards, I was wheeled into a room next to a burn victim.

A few hours later, I was supposed to be at a concert, which I could hear in the distance. Sting's concert. I was supposed to meet a friend there. Verona is a small community, and my friend had heard about me being attacked by dogs, so he brought me flowers at the hospital. However, he still went to the concert without me.

I went out to the balcony in my wheelchair, pulling IV tubes along with me. An Italian girl, Angelica, also in her twenties, was smoking and watching me. We started talking and she spoke some English.

"Would you lika a cigeretta?" she asked.

"No. Grazie, no fuma," (no smoke) I answered.

"Ahh, this cigarette a differentte," she replied.

I laughed as I could smell it was hash and tobacco. I went ahead and took a drag. Although I normally don't do drugs -- of any kind -- I figured after what I went through, it could only help the pain.

"Would you like a beera?" She asked

"Si," I answered with a smile and took a long drink. It was cold and refreshing. Angelica had a stash of beers next to her. We watched the concert in the distance at the Roman amphitheater, trying to make out the Sting songs.

Suddenly, there was a loud commotion and an Italian nurse came flying screaming down the hallway toward our peaceful balcony.

"Que cosa fai?" she screamed at me, grabbing the beer from my hand and scolding me in Italian all the way back to my room, as if I were ten years old. I looked back at Angelica who was watching with saturnine amusement.

The next morning, the doctor came in to check my leg and arm to see if they were healing. He had brought me a bottle of wine, chocolate, and some fashion magazines. He handed these to me and said in his broken English, "I heard you have been very bada girl."

"This is so you staya in bed. Stade." He said firmly gesturing to my leg.

I wondered what insurance plan would be cool enough to cover wine and chocolate. Then I thanked him and laughed as he fussed over the stitches. "You are modela and actressa? I hope you will not have the big scar on your gambina (leg)."

I smiled and thanked him again in Italian. The hospital staff treated me kindly and gave me extra pampering because I was so far from my family. It was actually the best hospital stay I ever had.

Later that week, Angelica was getting out of the hospital for her procedure and came to visit me with her friends before she left. They invited me to a wedding that would take place when I was out of the hospital. I did end up attending the wedding, which was near a beautiful lake. When I was finally released from the hospital, I was surprised that the bill was paid in full by a local Italian landowner who heard about my getting attacked. Since it was near his land, he wanted to pay the entire bill. All my food and stay at a local villa was paid for also. The young man from the hostel helped me and nursed me as I continued to recover. That kindness and compassion was the experience I had in Verona, Italy. And it's one I will never forget.

I eventually continued with my trip with a stop at the Greek Islands next but part of my heart stayed in Verona, Italy. I fell in love with the cobblestone streets, statue of Juliet, and Roman bridges. It is a beautiful town with amazing restaurants. From the first moment I was there, it felt like déjà vu, and I never got lost as I did other places. The piazza and gardens were lovely. Even the youth hostel was beautiful, an old villa converted with an aging unused fountain. The smell of fresh pastry and bread would fill the streets in the early morning as well-dressed residents who made their way to work. I traveled extensively in Italy, but this was one of my favorite spots.

It took an adjustment when I arrived back in the States. I quickly started working and auditioning again. I landed the understudy role of Lady Macbeth and got to perform it three times. I also had my first screen test and had landed a good agent.

I landed a walk on part for a European commercial featuring an American candy bar. My job was to walk by in my bikini as a young man sits at the boardwalk and bites into the candy bar. I arrived for a 5am call time, which included professional hair and makeup. Santa Monica is cold and grey, and I had to look as if I was romping in the sun on the beach.

A few days before the show, the wardrobe man took my body measurements.

"Ooooh girl, you are 37.5. 26. 37, you got boobies…" he exclaimed in a high pitch voice, laughing. I knew from his demeanor, he didn't mean this in a sexual way at all, and I laughed at his jokes.

"I am going to have FUN dressing you," he said and pulled out three different bikinis. I tried each one on as he examined me over his clipboard and finally selected the one for the shoot. I was allowed to wear my underwear under my bottoms. He was funny and shared with me about his previous life as a makeup artist and hairstylist to the stars, but he loved fashion better. He ended up giving me a pair of beautiful antique costume jewelry earrings to wear to an awards dinner. We struck up a friendship and he shared gossip about stars and his heartbreaks with some actors he had gone out with, who were still not open about their sexuality. In the '80s and '90s, it was still a stigma to be gay or bisexual and could impact getting work.

On another day before the shoot, I stood in the line of other bikini-clad women as members from the corporate board were visiting the shoot. One middle-aged German man looked me up and down and tapped my breast upward lightly, saying something crude in German. My fist had started to go up reflexively, but my friend next to me grabbed my hand and held it down. We would meet up sometimes to make some money and do extra work, then go have Damiano's pizza, finishing out the evening with Guinness and Celtic music at the local Irish pub.

Jenny whispered fiercely, "You couldn't punch that guy, although I want you to."

"I know," I said, "but he is a fucking creep."

"They all are, but let's get through this and get paid," said Jenny.

I sighed.

We were selected for the commercial and given instructions. The vignette was to be "romping" and playing volleyball. The day of the shoot, the Assistant Director yelled at some of the extras to look more enthusiastic in the windy, cold weather that the production company has lit to look sunny. No one was having fun, so everyone was actually acting for the next ten hours and "romping" for the cameras. During one break, someone gave me slippers and a robe with warm tea. I was grateful and exhausted by 7pm. Fábe came to pick me up, and I fell asleep in the car before we even got to Glendale, the other side of LA from Santa Monica.

Later that year, there was bad news in my family. My brother Michael's cancer had come back, but this time, it spread to his liver. It was a death sentence, but we had seen Michael beat cancer before, so we stayed in a comfortable denial. In 1989, Michael called me. He sounded out of breath.

"Hi, sweetie. I miss you," he said, taking a breath after each word.

I stopped what I was doing and sat down, "Michael, what is wrong?"

"Nothing, Honey. Well, I am having a little trouble breathing."

I was silent. His cancer had advanced.

"I am not feeling too well at all and sleeping on the floor, as we do not have a bed yet," he laughed, sharing this information with me. He and his girlfriend had been nomadic and exploring northern California since he ceased his treatments and quit his job.

I was still in my twenties, but I knew about Hospice and called the one in his town of Santa Rosa. They called him to begin services. I managed everything from Glendale via phone. I also called my brother Brent in Wisconsin, who said he would come out to see Michael.

"Bubber," I called Brent by his nickname, "he sounds bad." I cried while speaking.

Brent who is just over a year younger than Michael got emotional. He and Michael have had an intensely tight relationship their whole lives, and he loved Michael deeply. He gently talked to me before his wife Kathy jumped on the phone as well. I had grown up with Kathy; she taught me how to properly care for my horse and pets. She always read to me and loved me. Her gentle spirit always demonstrated her love and care. Even though she was quiet, she would stand up to my father when he said cruel things to me as a child. Just hearing her voice was a salve.

Hospice acted swiftly by supplying my brother a hospital bed in his home, and arranged for nursing care, oxygen, and coordinated prescribed pain management. They were compassionate and amazing. Hospice is one entity that always deserves support. They allow families to grieve with their loved ones at home, and the patient may choose to die without going to the hospital. I felt an enormous grief like I'd never felt before or since. My brother was young with a son, Andrew, whom he adored and was only a teenager at the time his father passed.

My mother, Brent and I cared for Michael for his last two months of his life. My grief was great, but my mother was facing the death of her first born son, and she was inconsolable. Brent had a deep connection with Michael and could not even remember life without his big brother. In the final days, my brother made time to say goodbye. When it came my turn, we sat and watched an old Star Trek rerun and held hands.

Michael said, "We have nothing to work out. You know how much I love you."

I responded with tears, "Yes, and you know how much I love you."

I leaned near him, and we just enjoyed our time. Michael had always made me feel loved. He gave me my boldness and confidence that my father tried to undermine.

The last day or so Michael played a final brotherly joke on me. It said everything about his humor and grace. We all surrounded him as he was dying, and he chose to be sitting on the couch. Michael was nodding off and we were all weeping, listening to classical music with candles glowing. Michael made a face at me when no one was looking and winked. It made me laugh. Everyone looked at me puzzled, then looked at Michael who had put his head down and closed his eyes. They looked back at me and he smiled. It was a funny moment between him and me, and Michael's way of saying "lighten up."

When we were young, he would also tell me when he was annoyed with my high energy level. "Tara, go play with the horse."

This would make me laugh when I was little and pestering him for attention. I still love to spend time with horses, and when I do, I remember my brother and his patience and love with such fierce grace.

We laid my brother's ashes to rest in the Pacific Ocean and I sang "What Is a Youth." As I looked out past the rock in Morro Bay, I thought of his spirit, free of pain and free, mingling with the ocean's half-light mist and the seagull's flight.

A month later, after my brother's death, I had an audition with the Globe Playhouse in Hollywood for an Equity Waiver production. I started my Anne from Richard the Third monologue. Then I froze. I had never frozen on stage; I had forgotten a line or two, but never just froze. The director was amazing and kind. He put up his hand and said, "Tara, I know your work, you have acted here before, it is okay. Tell me what just happened in your life?"

I answered slowly, "My brother died." It was the first time I had said it out loud.

He came over to me and embraced me as I cried. He looked teary eyed as well. "Okay. This is the thing; method acting is all well and good. There are some directors that say use your pain. However, I disagree. Use the pain of the character; your own pain can overwhelm you. Right?"

I nodded in agreement.

"Tara, we are going with an older lead, so you are not going to get this part," he says matter of fact.

I hung my head.

"Let's use this time to work past what just happened to you. You want to leave on a successful note," he said. He then told his assistant to reschedule the afternoon auditions.

I waited in silence.

"I am going to have you start again," he directed.

I did and stumbled; he encouraged me and made me do it three more times. At the end of my third try, he clapped and smiled. I will never forget his kindness and patience helping me sort through what could have become a habit of stage fright. I went on to perform again, and other than the usual butterflies that provide energy, I never froze again. I remember his Irish Wolfhound, his professor clothes and booming voice. I cannot remember his name, but he gave me a better gift that day than any therapist.

I did everything you are not supposed to do when you are experiencing deep grief. I gave up acting, changed careers to try politics, moved across the country and broke up with my boyfriend. My Political Science Professor encouraged me to apply for an internship in Washington, D.C., for Leon Panetta, who was then a Congressman.

I applied and got the position. I was very keen on animal advocacy issues and wanted to end horse slaughter. Most of my intern duties were making mundane copies and taking constituents on tours of the Capitol. I had no sense of direction and would get lost with my small groups, so I would improvise and take them down to the basement subway that was for the Senate and Congressional members and their staff. They would return starry-eyed comments after seeing a Kennedy or other famous celebrities. Panetta called me in and asked about this as his constituents were getting these special tours. I explained getting lost in the Capitol because I had a bad sense of direction and not knowing what to do. He laughed that booming laugh of his and waved me on.

Another intern and I had an intern lunch with him. We were able to ask him questions. The other intern asked about the Governor from Arkansas who was sweeping up attention in New Hampshire. Leon waved his hand and said, "That guy? Bill Clinton? He is just a snake oil salesman." He chuckled when he said it. The comment stayed with me, as years later Panetta worked as Clinton's Chief of Staff.

Leon told us his famous story of how he became a Democrat. Leon was working for the Nixon administration and was very passionate about civil rights. Nixon's staff told him to back off, but he did not. He said he walked into work one day and there was a press release announcing his resignation, that he was to read publicly. Leon said he went back home to Monterey County and decided to run as a Democrat, leaving the Republican Party. It explained why he was seen as fiscally conservative. I formed some new friendships and immersed myself into the work while in Washington, DC. I went back to California after the internship and worked on a Congressional race.

I had caught the political operative bug. I did not know where it would lead me.

CHAPTER 8

Washington, D.C.:
The Most Dangerous City on Earth

"As flies to wanton boys, are we to the Gods;
They kill us for their sport."

—William Shakespeare

I was excited to start my new life as a staffer for Joe Biden. I had no idea that what I thought was the start of my career would have an abrupt and ruinous end that would haunt me throughout my life. At that moment, I was happy and hopeful. My cat, however, was angry in her cat box under my seat. Cleo had been through all my many moves, men and a couple of Los Angeles earthquakes. She was loud, Snowshoe Siamese loud, with deep baritone meows of protest that were finally answered by the flight attendant half way into our flight from Los Angeles to Washington, D.C. The attendant came up to me with a fierce whisper, almost smearing her bright, red lipstick while she scolded me, "That cat is disturbing the other passengers." I shrugged.

She motioned for me to follow her. I gathered Cleo and my bag and followed her toward the front of the plane. We settled into the large grey comfortable seats, and my legs stretched out happily as Cleo, beside me in her cage, looked out. When they brought the filet mignon, being a vegetarian, I chopped it into tiny pieces for Cleo. She purred in approval and stopped the loud meows. I got interesting looks and glares from passengers in first class as I fed my cat the steak. Cleo settled in for the rest of the flight, quietly smug that everyone now knew she only rode first class. Just a few hours later, I watched out the plane window as we circled Washington, D.C. from the air, the night lights sprinkled across the outline of the monuments like stars.

Two months prior, I had made the same flight from California to Washington, D.C. for my interview with Joe Biden's office. The interview had come off the heels of my working a tough Congressional campaign in California as a Field Manager for Gloria Ochoa's campaign. There would be a third trip to drive out with my other cat, Othello and my car, once I knew I was staying for a while.

I flew in and met up with John Benito, whom I had known from my days as an intern for Leon Panetta. John was fun. He had great thick brown, wavy hair and lively, dark brown eyes. He was tall and well built. Everywhere we went, women of all ages stared at him. John's father was American and his mother Cuban. I had no idea the backstory of how the union came to be except bits and pieces shared with me from John, who told me that he loathed his father and adored his mom. John helped me drop off Cleo at my friend's house and took me to eat before the interview. I drank lemon water because I was too nervous for food. John wolfed down a plate of pasta and bread, catching me up on all I had missed since going back to California. We had sort of tried to have a relationship, but we were more friends with benefits. John was sweet, amazing and handsome, but neither of us felt the spark meant for romance. This went unspoken between us in our comfortable times together.

John grabbed my bag. "Okay, come on, chica, ándale?" He said this in mock American and Spanglish that made me giggle, swatting me to walk faster. John accompanied me all the way into the Russell building where I had to have the interview and waited for me.

The interview lasted all of twenty five minutes. This was a follow-up to the phone interview the month before. The Senator's scheduler, Marianne, pulled at her rim glasses and asked me questions that she had written down and said, "Several people have been in this staff position and either left or were… let go. Will you stay a while? What are your long-term plans?"

"I plan to stay for a while. Of course, I have long-term plans to be with your office, I hope," I answered, mentally editing my answer, wishing I had sounded more concise.

The Senator walked in as we talked. He glanced at me as he passed by. Marianne broke in, "Senator, this is Tara, all the way from California. She is interviewing for the staff position."

Joe Biden leaned over the desk and smiled wide at me. "Well, hi there, Tara. That's a nice Irish name," he says, offering his hand, "Joe Biden. Now, tell me about yourself."

"Umm well, I used to be an actress, and I got interested in politics in college. I worked as a campaign operative for a couple of campaigns in California and did an internship with Leon Panetta."

"Leon?" He asked, then nodded. "There's a good guy."

"Yes." I nodded as well, feeling suddenly shy.

He looked to Marianne. "Hire her," he said casually and walked out again with staff at his heels, vying to get a moment with him.

Marianne looked back at me, her eyebrows arched. "Well," she said and pursed her lips. "You are hired then."

I was stunned. I had never been hired at an interview. I asked for my start date and Louise, the office manager, asked me how soon I could move out.

As Marianne led me out, she shook my hand, "Congratulations!"

I floated out of the office and ran up to John furiously whispering, "I got it."

"What?!" he asked.

I kept us walking to the elevators not wanting anyone to hear. We rode to the first floor. We burst out the gold handled doors into the crisp sunshine.

"I got the job!" I shouted to John.

He hugged me tight then swung me around. "Let's go celebrate."

"Where?" I asked.

"Where everyone celebrates. New. York. City." He answered with a wink.

Bill Clinton had just blasted into the presidency. The first months were dazzling. As a Senate staffer, I had inaugural tickets. I met Maya Angelou, walked across the Bridge of Hope and danced all through the days. The night of the inaugural balls, I was dressed in my finest couture, picking my way through the streets with John. A limo pulled up alongside us.

A voice called out, "Hey there, you need a ride?"

It was Henry Winkler. I smiled and laughed; my shoes were getting ruined from the street. John and I piled into his car and breathlessly made small talk. It was less than five minutes to the first stop. Henry was going to a more exclusive event presumably to meet the President elect. I was very grateful Henry rescued me from worsening my new shoes and couture.

The night was magical with music and laughter. Hope was in every breath and every conversation.

As the months went on, I made my way every morning to work on the underground Senate subway, relishing my new life. I ate bagels at the *NYT* and dined at the hip Adams Morgan neighborhood restaurants with my friends.

As an intern for Leon Panetta, I stayed at a place affectionately referred to by locals as "the nunnery." It was an all-women's boarding dorm across from Congress. It was considered the safe place for parents to send their young women who were interning and working as staff on the Hill. We ate in a common dining hall, had gym-locker type bathroom/showers and no men were allowed upstairs after 8pm. It was secure and safe. Little did the parents, who unwittingly sent their young college grads here, know that the real predators were some of the members of the House and Senate. Remember, this is before Chandra Levy and Monica Lewinsky were part of our collective lexicon. This was a time in the 1990s when discretion was still on the side of the young princes who held office and allowed themselves to pillage as they saw fit without the nasty consequences.

One specific night, Washington, D.C. was still covered with a blanket of snow. All the public transportation stopped and the city was quiet with a glistening white sparkle. I had some friends from my new dorm meet outside. We walked in the snow and laughed. Then, we walked to a bar, drank beer and played pool. The snow was powdery at first, but as it began to slush, we chased each other in the closed streets with snowballs laughing and slipping. The night was the beginning for many of us just starting a project or internship and all of us from different parts of the country and world with the universal joy of a good snowball fight.

I met some of my best friends there, who also worked on the Hill. We had snowball fights on snow days, concerts and dressy formals to attend, heartbreaks and work challenges. We had secrets and were privy to sensitive information. Our conversations revolved around current events, love interests and what bill had a chance of passing that congressional session. Sundays in Washington, D.C. were filled with impromptu Frisbee and football games, lazy mornings stretching out to afternoons filled with coffee, NPR (National Public Radio), *The Washington Post*, naps and street fairs. I even reconnected with a couple of the women I met as an intern.

I treasured my Sundays. One such morning, I went around the corner to see my good friend, Suzy Lu, whom I adored, if only for her name alone. Suzy was from San Diego. I loved the way she constantly juggled/tortured three men who all vied for her. Suzy was cute, with straight black hair, petite and with a hoarse, deep voice. Men of all ages adored her ripped jeans and sexiness. Suzy had a rich papa and a plan. She was learning to speak Mandarin and was planning on working in the financial district with the Chinese markets. Her boyfriends were typically tragic, Bohemian poet, hip artist types with large features and intense affections for her, despite her capitalist focus. She rarely spoke of her love life, and I think only participated in the trysts out of boredom, as she was laser focused on her career.

We walked with Suzy's latest conquest, who trailed after us awkwardly like a puppy, to a nearby brunch spot in the Adams Morgan neighborhood. We would all meet for brunch and, at times, Suzy would bring one of her tragic boys with her. They were interchangeable, usually wearing a retro trench coat and absurd hat. They would sit sullenly ordering breakfast (usually something with egg whites) muttering about corporate waste as they ordered. During most brunches they would talk about their latest recycling project while trying to catch Suzy's eye to sense if they impressed her. After their attempts to join our conversations, they would finally leave. It was an endless source of amusement. Suzy seemed blissfully unaware of their despondent devotion and would march into the next topic after they left. Another friend, Stacey, and I would glance at each other after Suzy's latest boy made his exit and make the brush away motion, "Neeexxxt" giggling over our mimosas.

One day, after her latest conquest went into the bathroom, Stacey said, "Suzy, why do you always break these poor boys' hearts at brunch? It is sort of becoming a fetish."

Suzy would laugh and say, "Look, I am attracted to these types—the caring, passionate, quirky guys—for sex. They are so eager to please, but when they talk, it just becomes a problem."

She is wistful, "Someday I will meet a man that just knows how to please without a lot of conversation."

We all laughed.

Stacey waves at a male friend skating by, "Hey, see you later on?"

He skates up and pulls her onto his board, kissing her. She almost falls as she gets off but he catches her. We watch him weave in and out speeding away on his skateboard, his blonde hair flopping behind him.

Stacey takes a deep intake of breath; Suzy and I wrap our arms around Stacey's shoulders on either side, saying nothing as we walk on. We ended up at the flea market, and I bought a pair of earrings and a scarf that I never ended up wearing. We moved through the streets laughing, listening to street music as the afternoon sun warmed us. We would sometimes join a game of touch football or Frisbee on the capitol mall. Then everyone would head to a sports bar in Georgetown to watch whatever game was playing. Since we were all scattered from the many places across the country and the world, the teams playing would have some loyal fans.

We spent many weekends hanging out. We would shout and cheer and argue politics and international diplomacy over beer. Sometimes, we played pool or darts. Mostly, we just hung around and talked about current events. The afternoon would fade too quickly into evening, and we would have to prepare for the week ahead.

I remember these times with my friends because it was soon to be my last carefree weekend. My final innocence faded as quickly as the cherry blossoms that year. I started to settle into Joe Biden's office. I would go down to the basement for lunch, grab a sandwich and see members of Congress rushing votes through the labyrinth of tunnels.

One day, I had a craving for a good veggie sandwich. I was in a hurry waiting in line to order. I requested, "Could I please have avocado on my veggie sandwich?"

The woman behind the counter looked beleaguered and impatient.

"What is an avocado? We don't have that."

"Well," I explained, "it seems like it's a vegetable. It's green and tastes mild, not sweet. It is actually considered a fruit. "

She looked at me annoyed, "I said we don't have no avocados."

"Okay. It might be a good thing to have as they make good veggie sandwiches."

She looked at me now increasingly angry. "What do you want to order?" she enunciated each word.

"Okay, umm just a veggie sandwich, whatever you have."

She adjusted her hair net. I nodded back and looked behind me at someone laughing. The man was tall—John Kerry was obviously waiting to order, too, and I was holding up the line.

I finally received my soggy tomato sandwich and sat down.

John came by my table and asked, "Excuse me, where are you from? No wait. You are from California."

"I am! Wow, how did you know that?"

"Lucky guess," he answered smiling.

"And sorry I held up everyone. Nice to meet you, I am Tara."

He waved his hand as he and his aide walked away. "It's fine. Here's hoping you find that avocado."

When he would see me walking in the hallways or basement occasionally, he would say, "How are ya doing, California?"

I would giggle every time at this greeting. He never did say my name or chat with me. John Kerry was very friendly but also polite. He never had that creep vibe some of the other men had.

My first real introduction to the real D.C. came in the middle of one cold night. I got a phone call that I had to pick up a friend (as I was the only one with a car) from the outskirts of Virginia. Laney was wobbly, her blonde hair pasted to her head from sweat, drunk, had ripped stockings and smeared mascara from crying. She was standing waif-like on the side of the empty, dark road near the pay phone. She fell into my car verbally spilling out her story before she even closed the door.

"I love him. It was just a misunderstanding, you know?" She slurred and waved her finger at me in defensiveness. I took her back to our house as she sobbed. I was hoping she was not going to vomit in the car.

Laney had been having an affair with her boss, who happened to be a prominent, married Republican U.S. Senator. Apparently, Laney wanted more from him, and he unceremoniously deposited her on the side of the road in the middle of the night. The next week, heartbroken and scared, Laney left for home, leaving both her job and D.C. behind.

As I walked down the hall of the Russell building a week or so later, a staffer from that Republican Senate office stopped me and thanked me for my "discretion." Rolling his eyes, he called her "high strung."

I listened, said nothing, and moved on. I had sympathy for Laney but also a smugness that my life was not going to be some drama-fueled scene. I had seen enough of those in my childhood. I wanted my personal life to be normal and quiet.

Fate had other ideas.

I realize now that my world view at the time was part of the problem. I had been involved with Capitol Hill Women's Political Caucus and Hill Staffers for the Hungry and the Homeless as a volunteer.

Once in an elevator, another member of the Caucus argued with me about giving Ted Kennedy the award from us for his work with legislation to help women. She vehemently opposed it, and I accused her of being political.

Nell said, "Tara, I can't believe you are taking this stance. You have heard what they all do when they are out—Dodd, Kennedy and others. He fucked that girl in the cloakroom of the restaurant, drunk."

"Those are rumors," I answered, "and I heard it was consensual."

"Tara, that is not an excuse, it was disgusting. I was at the restaurant. I have seen them out more than once and how they treat women waitresses and staff," Nell replied, her face red with frustration. She and I were fiercely whispering our argument to each other. People swirled around us as we were locked in our exchange.

I knew she had a point, but I did not want to believe it. I had heard about what some of the male members of Congress did to staff and waitresses.

I shook my head and told her I had to go. "Look, just select who you want to nominate for the vote, and I will do the press release around it." I waved my hand dismissively as I walked out.

The idea that a Democrat could engage in sexual misconduct did not deter my loyalty one bit. Until it did. My denial was easy and part of the collective narrative that Democrats were above board and held the moral high ground on social issues.

I was not one for hanging out at bars a lot but Maeve and I would often go to the Dubliner to listen to Irish music and have a pint. Years later, Maeve and I would use Dubliner as a password to allow a reporter to talk to her. We were often working so much or Maeve back down at her college that we missed many of the hill staffer parties. However, one night, my friends got me to go out and it was a night that would change my life.

The party would prove more significant for me as I met my future husband there. As I walked in, I was wearing a simple forest green sweater and the silver crucifix my mother had given me from Malta. We went to the bar called Heaven and Hell. All the staffers were in Hell. I never made it up to Heaven. There was a water gun fight happening, and I got nailed in the forehead. I looked up annoyed that my hair had gotten wet and saw Ted. I grabbed a gun and fired back, hitting him with water. After we disarmed, he walked up to me and looked at the cross. Picking it up, he said, "Hello."

I looked back at my group of girlfriends who were whispering and laughing. Ted had thick, dark blonde hair and blue eyes that were fringed with beautiful long lashes. His body was sculpted and medium framed for his 6'4" height. The way he towered over me made me feel anxious yet safe at the same time. He gently took my hand and asked me if I wanted a beer.

I responded, "Yes."

He brought over the red, plastic cup as if it was crystal. He had elegance and a humor about him. I was completely taken with him. After the concert, we all shared a cab, and Ted walked me to my door, then he cupped his hands around my face saying how great it was to meet me.

"You're cute." he joked in his Midwestern accent. I smiled and felt a wave of hotness come over my face.

"So, who do you work for?" he asked.

"I work on the Hill," I replied curtly to this as I never like to say I work for Biden when out with friends. We all knew to be on guard from people trying to get gossip.

He laughed and said casually, "Yea, this is a staffer hill party, so I figured you work on the Hill."

I remembered and laughed embarrassingly. "I work for Joe Biden."

His eyebrows raised. "I work for a Congressman, Earl Pomeroy," he said smiling. "North Dakota, don't you know?"

"What do you do for Biden?" he asked.

"As little as possible." I replied dryly.

He laughed at this and later told me that he liked my response to his question.

We went on talking above the loud music until it was time to go. The girls were all at our security door to the house slightly tipsy yelling my name to come in. I turned to look at them, then turned back.

He wrote his number on my hand and then kissed me on the forehead.

"Until tomorrow then." he said slowly and dramatically.

My friends could hear our exchange and were already making fun of me and howling comments. Stacey missed the step that's not there and fell half way as two of the other girls caught her, and balanced her back on her wedge sandals into a standing position. This created more uproarious laughter.

I shook my head at Ted and shrugged, "Sorry, my friends are a little drunk."

He laughed and said, "It's all good."

With that comment over his shoulder, he stepped back into his cab to go home.

As we entered the house, the other girls were grilling me about Ted. They all agreed he was a hunk and unusually tall for D.C., the land of short bureaucrats.

"Oh. My. God," Kate said, slightly slurring her words, "He is so actual." We all rolled our eyes at her nonsensical statement.

She laughed drunkenly, and then said, "Umm, you are so going to marry him."

I sighed and said, "He says he works for a Congressman or something."

More laughter as we climbed the stairs. I made it back to my apartment weary from the week. As I lay down looking at the ceiling spinning from too much alcohol, I reflected on my life until dark sleep enclosed me.

The next day, I went to take a quick lunch break. I only had a few minutes to walk all the way across the Capitol Mall, order food and eat, so I was moving fast. Ted came up to me out of nowhere.

"Oh, umm, hi Ted," I said startled and stopped to look at him.

Ted smiled, handing me a bouquet of wilted wildflowers, "I just thought I would say hi."

I take the wildflowers from his hands. "Wow, thanks, how did you know I would be walking here?" I ask slightly puzzled.

"I kind of followed you…you did not call…but I normally would not follow anyone…but I don't have your number. I went to your office and they said you might be walking here."

He looked a little flustered brushing away his thick bangs from his forehead.

I laughed and said, "Okay. I appreciate the flowers."

We began walking in silence.

"Sooo, I was hoping maybe you would like to go somewhere to eat or go out sometime?"

I stopped to look at him. He looked back at me waiting.

"I am not into really dating or anything right now…" I trailed off.

He put his hand up, "Then just go out and have fun, no strings." He smiled.

I nodded. "Okay then, how about that coffee place near DuPont, on Saturday, then a walk to the Farmer's Market?"

He nodded in agreement, "Yeah, meet you about 10:30?"

"Sure, yeah. Sounds good."

"Okay, I gotta go back to work, cool, great, see you then." He awkwardly leaned in for a half handshake, half hug, then turned and jogged off.

Ten minutes later, as I walked past reception at work, both secretaries smiled when seeing my flowers and made teasing comments about "my suitor" as I whisked past them to the inner door and to my desk. Files had been added, and I had a scheduled meeting to attend for the Capitol Hill Women's Caucus, which

I was now late to attend. I hit my knee on the same spot I have so many times before on the inside of the low corner of the desk, trying not to swear from pain, as I grabbed my notebook to leave for the meeting room.

Later that evening, I reimagined my meeting with Ted. I really liked him. I liked his solid, midwestern voice and felt an instant attraction. I sank into the bath filled with lilac and rose scent. My candles lit and Etta James playing, I luxuriated while drinking my glass of wine. Then I imagine Ted's suggestions as my mind floated to desire, all languid in the water. I remembered his blue eyes and imagined his hands, what they felt like, and then just as I slid completely into my fantasy, crash! My cat raced in, knocked the candle into the bath, me-owed loudly, almost fell in herself, and scrambled to stay on her feet, as her tail slipped into the water. She screamed, running out of the bathroom in the wake of her destruction, as candle wax went all over the bathtub and me. My wine spilled and the mood was ruined. " Cleo!" I yelled. "Damn, I think this must be what it is like to have kids."

Saturday morning was warm as the sunshine filled my new apart-ment. I sat on my window deck with tea and the paper watching the people. Both of my cats were perched like gargoyles on each side of the deck watching the activity below. I drank the steeped tea with the slightest bit of honey. As I sipped and breathed the air, Stacey called me to ask what I was going to wear for the "date."

"It's not a date," I said back.

Silence.

"I am coming over," she said.

An hour later, "Girl, you are not wearing that raggedy-ass sweater to your date with Ted," Stacey announced as she walked in looking at me. The cats ran to greet her, and she petted each one and then kissed them.

"What is up with you? You know how to dress!" she scolded.

I rolled my eyes at her. "We are going to meet at the coffee place and then walk to the farmer's market. No big deal. Besides, this is my good ol' sweat-er. It's vintage."

"Hmmhmm," Stacy nodded, "Oh yeaaa…that is vintage alright. If it were anymore baggy, you could fit another person in it. Okay. Let's go into your closet."

Stacy strode to my closet, looking chic in her jeans, boots and short hair style. She pulled out three different shirts. "Okay, what about one of these?"

I sighed impatiently, "That one makes me look like my arms are big, and that one is too low cut. It sends a come hither message. Maybe this one." I put on a floral silk with a draped neckline. "There. Happy?" I asked while laughing.

Stacy nodded, unbuttoning the top button, which I buttoned back up. Then she put out her hand, "Give me that sweater."

"What? No! It's... I... I have had it for years," she somehow said with me in unison.

"You need a serious fashion intervention. Come on, you are working for a powerful Senator. Get some game on here." Our conversation continued for about another ten minutes. I ended up with a cuter outfit, makeup and my hair styled.

She sprayed me with perfume while I shouted, "Stop!" As we were laughing and running through the house, the cats running with us, she pretended to spray perfume towards my crotch. I shrieked at her, laughing.

"Stacy, oh my God, stop," I was laughing so hard I could barely breathe.

Stacy grabbed her purse and scrunched my hair.

"Okay, have fun on your non-date."

I looked in the mirror and rubbed off some of the makeup after Stacy left. She took my favorite old sweater with her. After rubbing off the eyeliner, I reapplied a more subtle line. I just didn't want to look like I was trying too hard.

Ted was already waiting at the coffee shop, and he looked very handsome.

"Hey, sweets," Ted says and his face lit up. I felt that happy feeling of a new infatuation. We sat and talked for an hour; then walked and continued to talk about our lives, the state of the world and our favorite music. We stopped at a park bench where he bought me a lemonade. As I sipped it, he watched me, then touched my curls. He brought my hair to his lips, then reached over to kiss me. It was a slow, soft kiss, and I liked the gentleness. I kissed him back, and we ended up staying locked in an embrace for quite a while. Pigeons fluttered around us. The start of our courtship was like most, tentative with missteps by both Ted and me. However, I was feeling insecure about myself due to the Biden office struggles and his presence, though peripheral, felt safe.

There would be some red flags I should have seen and maybe even a couple of flares. But what happened next with Joe Biden blinded me in a way to only seek escape and protection. It was from this place of vulnerability I made the mistake of staying with Ted. Later, after a baseball game and pizza, would come our first tangle. Ted had me on the inner stairs inside his apartment, his roommate not home. He was kissing me and had gone below me on the staircase so he could kiss the inside of my legs. I was not ready for intimacy and pulled away with my legs. He roughly got up and seemed insulted.

Ted said, "You do not let me close, I don't know if this will work out." His face was held in an expression of contempt.

I was stunned that my rejection of sex was a dealbreaker but then felt bad.

"It's not just tonight," he went on, "you seem to avoid intimacy. Are you seeing someone else?" He asked this matter-of-factly.

I assured him I was not, but he still seemed skeptical. I left his apartment feeling again like I had caused the problem by asserting what I wanted. This would only escalate later. My friendships and love life were happening at the same time I was dealing with the workplace issues and Biden's unwanted attention.

The Hallway

"Everyone sees what you appear to be, few experience who you really are"

—Niccolo Machiavelli

I was upset by the way Joe Biden touched me and treated me. The Chief of Staff had connections to the board of DuPont Corporation. The DuPont Corporation had many staff members who worked with Senator Biden. I was ordered to hire employees of DuPont's children (we called them "the trust funders") as interns. I met with the Chief of Staff and said I wanted to hire other qualified candidates and add diversity to our office. He insisted that half of the hires would be from DuPont employees' children. One of the young women I hired as an intern ended up having a dating relationship with a prominent staff member who supervised her. As they were both single, the ending was messy but not as bad as it could have been. And this is how it went on the Hill.

One day, my supervisor, for reasons unknown, called me into the office. My stomach flipped over wondering if it was the intern issue again, and what else I could have done wrong, as I walked in the room. There were raised voices among the staff present.

I was told that Senator Biden wanted me to "serve drinks at an event because he liked my legs and thought I was pretty." I was a former model and actress, so at the time such comments were of no consequence to me. I was asked to do many things based on my looks, and I did not know what value my intellect even held at the time, if any.

However, to a senior female legislative aide, it was not okay and she voiced her objection. Gen said, "You do not have to be treated like an object. You do not have to serve cocktails at a function for men because the Senator asked you to do this!"

The staff argued. I stayed silent and knew inwardly this was a huge problem, a trap, no matter what I did or said. I said nothing. I was later told by a supervisor to "keep my head down and fly under the radar, if I wanted to last." I was also told by Marianne, my supervisor at the time, to wear lower skirts and button up my blouse more.

Marianne's assistant had come to tell me that I was to dress differently. She was nervous and chewed her nails, holding up her hands. "Don't kill the messenger. You know how Marianne is, just try to stay on her good side."

I later confronted Marianne, upset by the charge that I dressed too sexy, as I wore normal clothes from Express.

"Just try not to look too sexy," Marianne said.

I was bewildered, as I did not think I looked sexy. If it was a thing, an issue, and somehow I was the problem, I felt like it was my entire fault. I felt ashamed.

As one problem was solved, my bigger troubles had just started. While at work, Senator Biden would touch me on the shoulder or rest his hand on my shoulder, running his index finger up my neck under my hair during a meeting. Again, I did nothing. It was uncomfortable, but I got used to it as he did this often to me. To others, he was also affectionate. I kept silent. I respected him, but I feared him.

Things at the office got hard for me, and it was obvious I was going to be forced out by legitimate or non-legitimate reasons. I was told by Marianne to be compliant, and she indicated that I should not make waves. The Chief of Staff just thought we were "all on our periods and complaining for no reason," Marianne shared with me.

As the days went by, I slowly lost more of my self-confidence and felt nervous at every task I completed for work. The retaliation had begun subtly, but then it became more pronounced.

Each day became a day that I might be fired because I had pushed back on not serving drinks at the fundraiser.

I called my mom. "Hi."

"Well hi, Honey, what are you doing?"

"Nothing, I just want to hear your voice."

Silence.

"Tara, what's wrong?"

"Nothing. God, mom I just wanted to say hi is all."

"That is all," she corrected me.

I laughed. "I use proper grammar when it matters, Mom."

"I can hear in your voice that something is wrong. "

I told her about Joe Biden.

"That nonsense stops today," she said angrily. "You march up to your supervisor and say, 'I want to file a sexual harassment claim immediately!'"

"Oh Mom, no, that just is not what can happen here, and it would not end well for me."

"Tara, promise me you will document this. And you will take action." She waited a moment before asking, "Tara?"

"Yes," I said, knowing not to argue.

We hung up, and I felt worse than before I had made the call.

Marianne said very intensely, "The Senator wants you to bring his gym bag. Now."

"Me? Why?"

Marianne thrust the bag at me, "Hurry, go catch up with him," she said urgently.

It was common for low-level staffers to run errands for the members of Congress. Once, I was asking what my friend was doing and she was walking Kennedy's dog, Blarney. She liked the dog but wondered if her B.A. in Political Science at an exclusive college was going to good use. The elite Democrats *talked the talk*, but in their offices, they often treated staff like servants. One of the lead legislative aides drove one of Biden's sons in a limousine to the Inaugural balls. It was considered a "volunteer" gig even though he had worked all day. It was as if all the discussion about class issues did not apply to the Members of Congress. I found it increasingly annoying.

I walked quickly, my heels clacking on the marble as I kept a clipped pace. The bag was heavy. *What does he have in this bag, a body? A Republican?* I laugh at my own joke. I wondered. Then saw him with his blue suit and light blue speckled tie combo.

"Tara!" The Senator grinned that 40-watt smile, reaching for the bag.

I felt a slight shiver. *Wolf,* I thought to myself. I was on edge around him, but I could not until this moment identify quite why.

"Here. Come here a minute, Tara,"

I was surprised he finally remembered my name twice in a row. A senior staffer shared with me she would shout his name on the Senate floor to get his attention before a vote, and it took almost two years for him to remember her name. He moved toward an inner hallway, his hand on my back.

My heart was pounding with an urge to run. I want *to run.*

This was my boss, and I needed to pull myself together and find out what he wanted.

"Yes, Senator?" I asked, trying to sound very formal but felt the tremble in my voice. It happened all at once, so quickly I was breathless.

One of his hands was on me, holding me in place against the wall. His hand was then running up the outside of my skirt then inside my skirt and all over. At one point his other hand cups my breast.

Absurdly, I wonder where the gym bag went. The damn crotch less panties I had worn for my boyfriend. His eyes widened as he touched me underneath my skirt. I felt shame and mortification all at once.

I tried to pull away, pushing his hands away. He grabbed me pushing me back, his knee separated my knees and I felt a sharp pain as our kneecaps clashed. He did not let go.

He whispered something in my ear, "Do you want to go somewhere else?"

As he is inside me with his fingers, he said low, "I want to fuck you."

The rest is lost in my frozen memory of this tangle. He started into a kiss, I moved my head away, disgusted by the smell of dry cleaning chemicals and mints and the touch of him. He was my father's age, in his late fifties and my boss.

It all happened quickly as I pulled away from his embrace. I wanted to say "Stop." I could not hear myself say it, maybe I did as I pulled away. He stepped back.

"Ah, come on man. I heard you liked me." I did not speak or cry out. I would not look at him as he pulled back visibly annoyed with a smile. His eyes were cold hard flints.

Since I started working there, I dreaded that famous temper and angry smile that did not go to his eyes. I started to leave, and he moved me back. I did not cry out as I was frozen with dread and just wanted to disappear. My throat and my voice wouldn't work. It was over. It was like a horrible storm. The whole event lasted just a few moments, but seemed longer because something inside me shifted or broke or both and became a hurt so deep, that it would stay with me for a very long time.

"You are nothing to me, understand? Nothing." He pointed his finger at me. His voice sounded quiet, steely and final. His eyes looked straight into me.

Then abruptly he said, "Go on now, you're fine. You are okay."

Instead, I was frozen in place. He lightly shook my shoulders.

I was dismissed. I felt dizzy. I could hear the echo of my father's voice telling me as he was kicking me again and again, that I was worthless.

"You are useless." I saw my father's face, a mask of drunken irrational rage, as he kicked at me and hit me. Nothing. I am nothing. I am trying to get my one shoe back on after being on my tiptoes when he was holding me at the wall.

The Senator adjusted his shirt and pants, and strode away with his gym bag. He did not look back. I heard someone shout, "Joe," but I could not see anyone. He was jovial in his response. And with that, Joe Biden was gone.

I shakily pulled at my skirt and pulled my bra back into place. I stood tall, my body shaking off the surrealness of the moment. I thought about what he said, that he heard that I liked him. *From whom? What did I do?* I reviewed the last few days in my head. *Had I given the wrong impression?* The humiliation that I had on lingerie under my work clothes in anticipation of seeing Ted burned my cheeks; the Senator's cruel words stabbed an old wound in my heart; and all of it made my head start to throb beyond my ability to think. I was cold. I was very cold to the bone, as if I caught a chill where my teeth could start to rattle.

My next memory was sitting on the marble stairs near the door. I had not gotten up in a while and had grown stiff. I made it home somehow and immediately took a shower. I scrubbed the dry cleaning smell off of me. The mint smell lingered around me like a bad taste. I lathered with my almond soap and scrubbed the day off me.

I put sweats on, grabbed all the clothes, including my shoes, and threw it all away.

I called my mother.

"Mom?" I said, and immediately I broke down as if I were a little girl again.

"Honey, Tara, what happened, what is wrong?" Her tone was concerned and frantic. She knew this was about to get real.

"Mom, something happened, I am okay. It's okay but…," I blurted in between tears.

Stating the obvious, "You do not sound okay," my mom said.

"Mom, the Senator, he… he put his hands all over me and inside me," I started sobbing.

Hearing my own words state it out loud, made the reality stone cold true with no room left for denying what happened, even if only by checking out.

"Tara, what? Call the police right now, keep on what you are wearing. Do not shower. Call the police," she commanded.

"No, mom, I can't do that. I would lose my job. I would lose everything," I defended.

"Tara, that is assault," she emphatically stated.

We talked for a while longer and my mother ended up sobbing when I would not go to the police.

She called me again an hour later, soothingly but deeply sad.

The next day, I called in sick and stayed in bed. I felt sick, and my knee hurt. I called Maeve and told her, sobbing through the whole story. She calmed me down and agreed with me not to go to the police.

I called Collin. I told him, while crying, that I may lose my job and shared with him the incident. As he was still living with our mom at the time, he had heard her wanting to call the police and knew there had been some drama.

"Love you, Tara, Come home," he softly pleated.

I laughed through tears and said it may be sooner rather than later.

After the weekend, I mustered up the courage to go back to work, and the office was humming along as if nothing happened. Everyone thought I had been sick. No one asked. I was quiet and subdued.

Christine, the receptionist noticed my absence.

"Oh, Tara," she said, "I miss your smile, you were so enthusiastic when you first came here." She wrote down her home number and said, "Call me if you want to talk."

I never did call her as I did not know who to trust.

I did, however, go to report the sexual harassment to the appropriate department, which required some counseling process. I filled out the intake and handed back the form. I was told that someone would call me.

A few days later, Ted had come up behind me and wrapped his arms around me which lifted my boobs. I pulled away annoyed.

"Just stop!" I snapped at him, "I…"

He drew back surprised, "Wow, what is up with you tonight?"

I shook my head and turned up the CD playing Phish drowning out his questions, and distractingly said, "Sorry, bad day."

"I'll say," Ted replied, as he had not yet seen my snappy side.

I didn't care about trying or being nice with my mood just foul.

Ted sighed deeply and said crisply, "Look, maybe I should go."

"No," I responded. "I'm sorry," and I went to hug him, "I was just… I don't know."

He shrugged and was still distant. We ate and continued to listen to Phish. In bed, I clung to him and for the first time since we started going out, we did not have sex.

Ted whispered, "Are you okay?"

I started crying, and he hugged me tighter to his chest. He did not ask me any more questions.

I felt frustrated. *How did I get here? Why had I not confronted the Senator and stood up for myself? Why was I becoming so weak and timid?* I was audacious and should have stood up for myself.

Maeve and I sat quietly on the lawn on the Capitol Mall sipping coffee. "Okay, so the Senator is still acting weird toward you."

I was almost whispering, "Yes. No. I don't know. After the hallway, he looks straight ahead and just does not acknowledge me. People will not talk to me or greet me the same way. It is like I am frozen out and somehow they know I filed that paper."

I continued, "You know, I wanted to talk to someone about him running his hand up my arm, coming behind me during meetings and..."

"And what?"

"Okay, like running his finger up the back of my neck while we are at the Intern meeting."

"Tara, what the hell? How often does that happen? And what he did to you?"

"Once in the hallway. A few times everything else."

Maeve draws in a deep breath, "You need to go to your supervisor."

"I did, three of them. They kind of blame it on me. They said I need to dress differently, more conservatively, and even wrote me up. I am now stripped of my duties and Denis told me my job was to find a job, that I am not a good fit. I am so distracted and afraid I am making mistakes." A tear rolled down my face. I hung my head ashamed, as I felt like I was failing in life.

Maeve pulled herself up off the lawn, "Tara, that is bullshit. There are laws that protect you."

"Not as a Senate employee, it seems. There are different rules."

Maeve shook her head in frustration.

I told her about the hallway incident again with Joe Biden as I did on the phone the day after it happened, but I broke down again into tears.

Maeve sat near me absorbing the full account of what happened and rubbed my arm, "I am so sorry this happened to you. What can I do?"

"Nothing. I...just listening. I am good," I replied brokenly.

"Have you told your mom?" Maeve asked.

"Oh, you can imagine. I am telling her in bits and pieces. She is furious and wants me documenting everything. She wanted me to go to the police. But really, the Capitol Police? They protect them, not us."

"She's right, but I see your point. It is actually dangerous. Jesus. I would keep quiet too."

"It is just such bullshit how women are treated here. I mean wanting me to serve cocktails to a bunch of rich donors...men...'cause he likes my legs and thinks I am pretty and touching me and the rest," I continued angrily in tears.

"God, I remember when you first told me that. I knew you were in trouble then," Maeve responded, looking at her hands. "Those men just assume that is what we are here for, their amusement. I suppose it is the same for you white girls."

I nodded.

"Okay, so you got to stand up and be heard through the process of the complaint?"

"I will lose my job, and maybe my career." I replied.

"You may get justice. He cannot move people around for his pleasure."

We looked at each other knowingly.

"I am too scared one day, mad the next. None of this is how I thought it would be," I replied.

Maeve bowed her head. We sat quietly. She patted my hand in comfort.

"I used to be audacious. I went on adventures. I went to Europe and traveled alone," I said with effort, my voice was higher.

Maeve nodded.

"Look at me. I am afraid of making Ted mad and of his temper. I am walking on eggshells at work. I am afraid to just call out Biden and what that would mean. It is almost like I was more myself when I was younger. You know?"

Maeve remained silent. I wanted to lift the heaviness of this conversation and stop thinking about what happened.

"Did I ever tell you about Yugoslavia?" I asked.

"What? Yugoslavia?" Maeve answered, "No," she said while laughing.

"Well, once upon a time, I was a solo backpacker who decided to travel through Europe for the early spring and summer. I was in Italy, and I met an Italian boy named Stefano. It was such a wild time in my life traveling through Europe with no strings attached," I began and I sank into the memory of Stefano and Italy, narrating the scene for Maeve.

I reached over and brushed the pastry crumb from Stefano's lip as I kissed him. I whispered to him. He opened his eyes knowingly, his long eyelashes dark and slowly closing. I had actually met him near Stubai, a glacier skiing in Austria when we decided to meet up.

"Aspetta un momento," he said. "Aspetta" he repeats in Italian.

He ran out of the shop and came back with a basket. He purchased some drinks and sandwiches from the shop to go.

"Adiamo," he said to me with a smile, then in English he said, "It is a surprise. I think you like."

He winked. We then got on his motorcycle. I had no idea where we were going. We were young and infatuated with our freedom. We ended up in Trieste, Italy, and then we crossed a border into what was then former Yugoslavia.

We saw the craggy hillsides sprinkled with olive trees and cypress as the cliffs edged the sea. It was a beautiful day. We stopped and had some local wine and fresh bread with olive oil. Stefano took me to a lovely vista overlooking the sea, and no one was around. He carefully laid out the blanket with our picnic. We ate and talked, bridging the English and Italian. He brushed his dark blonde hair from his face and asked if he could kiss me again. I smiled, feeling suddenly shy, and nodded. We enjoyed our vista and then slept in the warm sunlight with only birds and the sounds of the sea. After a while, he said we should get back into Italy. Then he stopped suddenly, and looked pale with a realization.

I asked, "Che fai?"

He hit his head with the palm of his hand, "I forgot you do not have a Visa, you are an American, and we have to get back through the checkpoint."

I felt uneasiness but brushed it off thinking it would be fine. I knew I looked worried though, even as Stefano said it would be no problem.

"Hey, usually they wave through Italians without questions. Just say nothing, okay? Va Bene? Niente! Okay? I am so... so sorry, carina."

I answered him, "Yes. Yes, si, si I will say niente."

I got on the back of his motorbike, and we sped off towards the checkpoint at the border. Then we saw the Yugoslavian booth with the flag. A few yards ahead was the Italian checkpoint with the Italian flag. I held my breath, hoping for the best outcome.

The Yugoslavian guard acted as if he had won the lottery. Here I was, an American girl, no passport or any identification. The guards sent Stefano on, and I was to be detained. He tried to protest, but they said if he argued, he would be detained as well. He left, head bowed, telling me that he was going to find a lawyer and call the consulate. I sighed and inwardly remembered my older brother Michael chiding me when I engaged in impulsive behavior. I guess going with a boy I barely knew, on a motorcycle, to a foreign country, without my papers would qualify as impulsive behavior.

I was cold and hungry again as I waited on the dank, cement bench at the checkpoint. Two Yugoslavian guards with automatic weapons stood vigilant. Two men strode in and sat down in front of me. One had a uniform similar to police. One man was in regular work clothes with a tie, but with a gun attached to his hip, and a pager. He looked at me calmly. He had slight freckles, light strawberry blonde hair, and was at least a decade older than me. His lips were full and he had bright eyes. If I were in a different situation, I might have found him attractive. The two men spoke Slavic to each other. Then, I heard a word or two I recognized. I decided to speak up.

"Are you Russian? Please, I speak English. My name is Tara Reade, and I am American. Nice to meet you." I said part of it in Russian.

The blonde one looked up quickly, "You speak Ruskie?"

"No, only a few words."

I looked at the blonde. He did not tell me his name, but he stared at me in a very intense way. In slow English he asked, "Tara. OOOOkkkaaayyy." He then asked, "What makes you come to Yugoslavia?"

His English was broken but I could grasp it. I sighed and said I was on a picnic with Stefano, my friend. They did not understand the word picnic. I did not know it in their language, so I said "mangia" in Italian or "eat." The two men had an intense exchange in their language or Russian. I heard Stefano's name brought up several times. There was some dispute as to why Stefano was gone and not held there.

The Russian officer looked back at me, "Where is your passport?"

I answered that my passport was at the hotel in Italy.

"What hotel?" he asked quickly, and I told him.

"Let us call."

My eyes filled with tears. "I did not know to bring my passport," I whispered.

There was more talking between the two men. The blonde sighed deeply and rolled his eyes. There was a long pause and a discussion in Yugoslavian or Russian, then I heard some Italian. It was a linguistic mess. I heard the name of the town, Trieste and Verona.

"Okay. I take you and escort you to hotel. You show me passport and verify, yes?"

My heart pounded hopefully with joy. Later, I realized he probably would have been overwhelmed with paperwork and this was the easiest way to send me on my way and not deal with an international incident involving an American consulate.

"Yes. Yes, anything you say," I replied.

"Then, we will decide if further action will be taken," he finished.

I was quiet again. He escorted me to his car. The long car ride was quiet except when he asked how I know Russian. I answered that I just looked up a few words. It is too hard to discuss my childhood friend.

I was tired and hungry. I felt nervous and weepy. He saw the worry on my face. I looked out the window at the dark night. He was quiet, then said, "I am sorry…." He couldn't find the rest of his sentence in English. I nodded my understanding. He patted my hand and then took it and kissed it in a gentlemanly fashion.

We stayed quiet, and I drifted into a light sleep as he drove. He nudged me and asked me again for the name of the hotel. We stopped for petro, and he sorted out the rest of the trip. When we arrived at the hotel, I went to the front desk and asked for my passport out of the safe.

The hotel clerk said, "A Mr. Stefano was looking for you earlier and left this note." The blonde looked at me and smiled slightly. I sighed and handed him my passport.

"Take me to your room now," he said, his tone commanding.

I must have looked worried as he said, "I must inspect to make sure you are honest about this being your room."

"Okay," I muttered wondering about my rights; then, I remember he was doing me a favor by not having me processed into the government of Yugoslavia for illegal entrance.

We entered my room; I turned to him and said, "It's messy, sorry."

He looked back at me blankly not understanding the word.

My backpack was in disarray and laundry in a pile. He shook his head and shrugged. He looked at my backpack, checked the pockets and said, "Okay, we are done here. Thank you. I will make this, umm, photo of your identification. You may not return to Yugoslavia without proper identification. Do you understand?"

I understood he meant a copy, but I did not correct his English.

I nodded. I was relieved and had no intention of returning to Yugoslavia.

"Good," he responded. "I will be right back with your passport."

While he was gone, I organized my backpack and cleaned up. I changed into some shorts and a clean shirt. I heard a soft knock. He stood in the doorway.

"Here is passport."

"Thank you," I said, taking it back.

He looked at me intensely and put both his hands on my waist, holding me in front of him. He was my height, maybe shorter.

"My name is," he started to say in Russian… then he stopped.

I looked at him, a bit worried and anxious as to what he would do next. He abruptly let go of me, paused, turned and said, "You are quite pretty. You need to be more careful. You should not be going on motorcycles with boys. Be safe now with your travels."

I nodded and said thank you in Russian, and then good night. He smiled slightly and shook his head, then left. He never did tell me his name. I closed my door, relieved that I was back in my warm hotel room. I knew his kindness and even the drive back to my hotel room was probably to avoid the paperwork and diplomatic issue of detaining a young American woman.

I ordered room service, took a bath and watched an Italian drama. As I was about to drift into sleep, I thought about the Russian's vivid eyes, his accent, and silently said a prayer of thanks that I remembered a couple of Russian phrases. Years later, Yugoslavia was torn by civil war, and over 130,000 people died, according to human rights reports. I wondered what ever happened to the Russian who was kind to me, or if he was able to get home to his own country. As sleep took me, I realized I never called Stefano to let him know I was back and safe.

Maeve laughed and said with exasperation in her southern drawl, "One, I cannot believe you did not end up finding out more about the cute Russian. And two, I cannot believe you went to a foreign country with no papers. Good golly, Miss Molly."

I laughed at the outdated expression.

"I know, I know, I don't advocate traveling around without identification that is not what I mean. I was just bolder. I was sort of more spontaneous and fun instead of cowering at my desk afraid that the next mistake I will make will mean my last day on this job because I am reporting a Senator for what he did," I said vehemently.

Maeve nodded, and we were quiet for a while. She chuckled again and mocked a swat at me, "Yugoslavia... girl?"

"What can I say? The folly of youth and an Italian boy on a motorcycle…," I sighed.

We laughed again and started to get up from our place on the vast lawn of the Capitol.

Maeve stretched, "Dinner at my house? We can watch a movie and drink wine, have popcorn, eat chocolate?"

I smiled, "Absolutely, all the food groups."

I tried to seem jovial. But my heart was still heavy with anxiety about what happened with Joe Biden and the shame that followed me. We stood and watched a flock of geese flying and airplanes dart across the sky as the afternoon light faded.

The following weeks grew harder than I would imagine. I was still in denial about losing my career and though I could get another job on the Hill, I would not. In fact, once word had gotten out behind the scenes about me filing a complaint, there were negative whispers about me everywhere.

The final meeting before I filed the sexual harassment complaint was with Ted Kaufman, Chief of Staff. He had a mug and legal pad.

"You asked to see me?" Ted Kaufman asked.

"Yes. I mean there is something I want to talk about. It is about Senator Biden."

Ted looked at me coldly and silently. He reminded me of a reptile that hardly blinked. Then he wrote something.

I stuttered through my complaints and asked for it to stop. I almost discussed the hallway but lost my nerve again.

He stared at me. "Thank you."

I waited and he nodded, gathering his notebook. I was dismissed. I left shaking, as he was intimidating.

One day it happened, Dennis Toner asked to see me. He moved me into an office by myself with no windows, just a door and an exit.

"Your job is to get a job," he said firmly. "You will no longer speak to the interns or the staff, and Marianne is no longer your supervisor."

"I want to talk to Ted Kaufman," I answered.

"This is our decision, and it is just not a good fit. You have a month to find another job."

"What are my duties now? What do I put on my resume?" I asked.

"Special Projects," He answered curtly. Then adds, "Oh, and you will report only to me. Check in every morning, and tell me when you leave."

He left as I looked at my cramped surroundings. I felt ashamed and angry that I lost my job duties. I felt hot tears starting in my eyes but tried to hold them back.

I would again see Joe Biden in the hallways after the assault. Instead of his usual smile and wink or nod to me, he looked straight ahead as if I were not there.

The last time I saw him in person was at an intern meeting he attended briefly.

He came up behind me and placed his hand on my shoulder firmly, his fingers underneath my hair. I froze and felt sick and perplexed. At this point, I knew I was being fired. I called my mom later and described the scene.

"Mom, why did he do that? I asked.

"Tara, that is how he establishes power over you and dominates the room." She explained. I sighed.

I volunteered at the Robert F. Kennedy Memorial and met wonderful people. I was in charge of the VIP tent flow and got to meet interesting people who attended. I continued my volunteer work as I looked for jobs.

I was not sure anyone would call me after the complaint. I began to think I had to leave Washington, D.C. so I started looking for work in California.

During one of my last days, I sat morosely on the stairs after work. I was having a difficult time and felt nauseous and shaky. It had hit me that my career dreams were ending.

Sean, the security guard stopped in front of me, "Hollywood," he asked, "Whatcha doing out here?"

Sean had always called me Hollywood since I worked as an intern for Panetta. He would say, "Hollywood, you should be back in California in movies. What are you doing in this old gloomy place?"

He would laugh and hand me back my ID badge as we made small talk at the security entrance. His upbeat banter always made me feel better, even on the crappiest D.C. days. This time, I did not smile.

Instead, I just looked at him and though I am not sure how I looked, he seemed concerned. "Hey. Hey you okay?"

"I don't know. No." I was close to tears.

I looked behind me at the hallway, and he followed my gaze.

"Did something happen to you?"

I shook my head no, but I knew he did not believe me. He got up and went for his walkie-talkie. I heard the scratchy static as he and his co-worker talked back and forth in code slang. He looked down at me worried. I was getting a headache and felt nauseous. Sean helped me to my feet saying softly, "Hey there, let's get you home."

I looked him in the eyes. He looked sad, too.

"Look, my man Thato is going to pick you up and take you home. Okay?"

I nodded and walked, my legs wobbly from the cold and sitting. I took his arm as we went to the street. A few minutes later, a cab pulled up.

Thato and Sean exchanged greetings, "How are you, Bro?"

"Good, you know, getting along and going where I shouldn't be going." Thato let out a booming laugh.

"Who do you have here?"

"Oh, this here is Hollywood. She had a bad day and needs a ride home. You know how it is," Sean answered.

"Mmmmhmmmm." Thato responded looking at me. "I have had my share of bad days."

I climbed into the taxi and saw the colorful Rasta beads and decorations. Reggae filled the cab, and Thato turned to me, "I am from South Africa, not Jamaica."

I nodded, as I had not said anything.

Thato went on to say how passengers assumed his accent was from the Islands and how the Capitol was a "malhus."

"That means crazy house in English," he explained.

He was older, with dark skin, and white hair sprinkled through his beard. His presence was comforting and brought back a sense of normalcy to the day. I realized I didn't have my purse.

"Oh," I say, "I don't have my purse. But I have some cash up in my room I can get."

Thato waved his hand, "No way. No, this is for my bro, Sean. He calls and I help the situation."

For the ten-minute drive, Thato makes small talk about Reggae and driving a cab. We pulled up to my street, and he stopped and turned.

Thato handed me his card. "Today you got yourself a guardian angel. I will pick you and your friends up anytime. Just call. And especially late at night. I get you all home safe. You know, there are very bad things that happen here."

I nodded, wishing I had been with a guardian angel about two hours ago.

"I see your face, miss. You have a better day now and don't let your mind dwell on those bad people up at that place. You don't belong there, I can see. I know, I see things. You gonna find yourself a better place. Ask me, I see when there is bad trouble."

He looked at me, his brown eyes very serious. I shook his hand and smiled for the first time that day. He smiled back, wide, revealing two gold crowns.

"You take care, sister. It's all gonna be okay. Maybe it is not okay, not today, but someday all this mess will be behind you now. And keep my card."

I looked at him, wondering if he was truly an angel on earth, flown in from South Africa for safety and comfort.

"How did you know it was bad?" I asked him.

Thato chewed reflectively on his toothpick.

"Oh, that place, I pick up broken hearts from that place a lot. That place got a darkness and a light, you don't ever know which is coming on what day," Thato said, looking over his hood.

I sighed, "You are a wise one."

He laughed at this, and we shook hands again. I wished I could hear more of his stories, but my head was splitting with pain.

I got out of the taxi, grateful for the uplifting words and went to my room. Thato watched as I went into the building. I still smelled the dry-cleaning solution and even sniffed my clothes to see if it was me, it's not. It bothered me.

I called my mother. Then exhausted, I stood in the shower, using my almond soap until the hot water turned cool.

Ted comes over with take out. I buzzed him in while wrapped in a towel. 'Tara. You hungry?" He shouts into the hall as I am dressing into my sweats in the room.

"No, I'm good."

"Oh, huh," he replied sounding surprised, "I got you your favorite, Kong Pau veggies."

I went in and poked through the boxes listlessly.

The last time I spoke to Joe Biden's office was months later on the phone after moving to Morro Bay, CA. I was fixing sauce for spaghetti over the stove. My daughter, Michaela, was a baby in her little chair.

The phone rang, so I threw the kitchen towel over my shoulder and grabbed it.

"Hi, Tara? This is Jack O'Connell's office," a male voice answered on the line.

"Yes?"

"Umm...we ran into a snag with a reference. I am really sorry to say this, but we cannot go forward with the hire at this time. You did great in the interview, I want to assure you." He paused.

"Who gave me a bad reference?" I asked.

"Well, ahh, we heard from Joe Biden's office."

"Would you do me a favor and give me a few minutes to straighten this out?"

"Well, sure, okay. We are here until 6pm tonight."

"I will call you back." I felt a flush of anger and tears of frustration as I went to get my address book from the drawer. I dialed the numbers furiously and asked for Dennis Toner. I was put immediately through to him.

"Tara," Dennis sounded surprised and said my name as if we are friends and liked each other. We did not.

"Dennis, I am living here with my husband and baby in Morro Bay, CA. I was applying for a job with State Senator Jack O'Connell, and you gave me a bad reference?" I almost shouted the last part. "That was not our agreement. You said I was to get another job. And may I remind you, I filed a sexual harassment form?"

I was now so upset that I was almost in tears. Michaela heard my voice and cried. Immediately, my breast milk soaked through my bra pads. I sat down and nursed Michaela while still yelling at Dennis. The call ended with Dennis saying he would call back Jack O'Connell's office within the hour.

"Hi again, this is Jack O'Connell's office."

I had since put Michaela down for a nap as I prepared a salad when I received this second call. I chopped up the red peppers with the phone crooked in my neck, resigning myself to being told I did not get the job.

"We would like to offer you the position."

I stop chopping.

"What?" I asked, amazed.

He laughed, "Well Biden's office called back and said they misspoke and gave you a glowing reference. Jack and I agreed that anyone that can get his office to call back that fast deserves the job. Can you start Monday?"

"Wow. Of course."

I hung up the phone relieved, as Ted had lost another job and was currently unemployed. There was rent and diapers and health insurance that still had to be paid. Ted came inside from smoking pot. I do not smoke pot; never did because it does not interest me and especially during this time as I was nursing. The times I tried it, it made me feel anxious and hungry, so I just did not smoke. I did not care that Ted smoked pot, except when he got unmotivated. Ted immediately sat down in the kitchen.

"Where's dinner?" he asked. I smiled back.

"We are celebrating. I got a job."

He looked relieved and stretched.

I looked at my daughter feeling happy but anxious because I would have to leave her all day so soon. She slept peacefully, her apricot skin soft as butter as I stroked her cheek. My mother volunteered to watch Michaela so Ted could look for work. Also, I was nervous to leave her alone with him after he had shaken her one day and became so unstable. He also would hit the wall sometimes in frustration when she cried a lot. I did not feel comfortable with him watching her.

As I started my duties at Jack O'Connell's office, I got a stern warning to not bring Michaela to Children's Day on the Plaza after someone told them she was there. Children of staff could not be seen at events. I had been there giving a speech and handing out certificates for Jack.

My mother held Michaela and pushed the stroller, and I was wearing a red suit. The Saturday morning was crisp, and as I gave Jack's speech, the media showed up. My breast milk came in again, and to my embarrassment, my shirtdress had dark stains. I put the certificates I was holding and the lectern in front of me trying to hide the stains coming through as I needed to nurse. It was a challenge working for Jack in this way as he was old school in that staff were to have no life. We worked salaries and so worked weekends with no pay (it was volunteer) and children were not to be seen. It made me sad to always leave Michaela behind with my mom or Ted on weekends for ridiculously low attendance events. However, as in Washington, D.C. many Democrats treated their staff like low-level servants. The reward was proximity to power.

CHAPTER 10

Defying The Rule of Thumb

For centuries, in our nation and abroad "wife beating" was, and still is, an accepted practice. The long-standing legal concept of "rule of thumb" allowed a husband to beat his wife with an instrument no thicker than his thumb.

The Violence Against Women Act, passed in 1994, provides survivors of domestic violence with the legal protection they need and deserve to escape the cycle of abuse. If you or someone you know needs resources for victims of domestic violence, visit the National Domestic Violence Hotline (nvdh.org) for a directory of support services in your area

– Ed.

I had a dream more than once that my daughter and I did not survive. It was actually a dream within a dream. In it, I am suspended above looking down at a horse-drawn wagon that carries the dressed skeletal remains of my daughter and me. I always feel terrified, suffocated and unable to scream all at once.

A calm, invisible voice next to me says, "You know you never got out. Your spirit has not accepted this, and all that you think you remember since that time is something you made up in your mind to create comfort because you could not accept your own death."

I always wake up sweating and shaking. Panic drifts to relief. I feel myself awake and alive. I maneuver myself from bed, heavy limbed and numb.

Seattle 1999

I continued to plod through my morning routine of making coffee, letting the dog out and waking Michaela for school. I felt the fogginess of a dream hangover, which then shifted to gratefulness as we faced the new day and all the wonder it could hold for us.

Let's just start in the middle. In 1999, with the help and advice of law enforcement and domestic violence advocates, my daughter and I got a sealed name change and social security change. We were moved to Seattle to start a new life and accepted into the New Beginnings program, which helped us in many ways. We were able to get counseling, and I was able to secure work and housing. Michaela began a normal routine with school. Seattle in the late '90s was rated one of the best cities for children. Michaela and I would go rainbow hunting, take ferries to the islands, go to parks and make new friends. I came to Seattle with $50, and it was spent on Michaela.

I took her to the FAO Schwartz where she saw the tall lava lamp-like structure filled with Barbie shoes two floors high. Even as an adult, it was pretty awesome to see that. She picked out her own Barbie, and we went to eat on Capitol Hill where she could order her meal.

The server smiled and said to Michaela, "Well, hello, Miss Thang, you look fabulous. Oh, my god look at those curls. Bennett come here, look at the curls on this one."

Another server, Bennett, came over smiling, and they were friendly and kind. I felt comfortable.

Michaela explained to them that she needed three cherries for her Shirley temple.

The server looked at me, "What are you having, Mama?"

I shook my head no, "I am good."

He came back with a lovely salad and sourdough bread.

He whispered, "For you, honey, and do NOT even think about a tip."

You are a queen here, ma'am, always."

The warmth and friendly first meal was a wonderful introduction to the Emerald City.

The restaurant and shopping provided a normalcy for Michaela after her difficult goodbye to her Nana. We left a lot of her things with my mom. I will never forget, as the train in San Luis Obispo pulled away to LA, how Michaela sobbed for my mom. My mother had done her childcare whenever I worked, so they had bonded. My mom had a very loving and gentle relationship with her. Mom was tougher on me growing up, but there were different dynamics now. Michaela and my mom connected on art and loved to take their walks. When we landed in Seattle, we were taken to a confidential domestic violence safehouse. It was in a neighborhood but had a gate with security cameras and an enclosed yard. However, most homes and apartment buildings in Seattle had gates and security cameras at this time. It was a rambling house with lots of room. It did not feel institutional. When we arrived, I had paperwork to fill out. The advocate showed my daughter around and asked what she liked to play with.

"I like to draw with my Nana and read with my Mama," she answered hiding behind me, not wanting me out of her sight.

We decided to hold off on the intake interview until we were able to put Michaela to sleep. I filled out forms while Michaela played with some trucks and colored. I ushered Michaela to the new bedroom we would share and tucked her in with books and songs.

"Mama?" She asked, "Why are we here with all these people?"

"We are going to live here now, and you will go to school. At least while we look for our own special place we will live in soon," I answered.

Michaela played with her Beanie Baby cat while rubbing her eyes.

"Will Nana come?" she asked.

"Of course. She will come and visit," I answered.

"Now, tomorrow we are going to explore parks. I read that Seattle has the best children parks in the whole country."

Her eyes got wide. "Parks with ponds and ducks?"

"Yes, for sure there will be ducks," I smiled.

I lay with her as she fell into an exhausted sleep from the very long day. I went to see the advocate. She was young, maybe early twenties.

"I know you have had a long day. We just need some of the emergency forms in and the confidentiality forms signed.

"Your daughter is so adorable. We get free tickets to the Wallingford Park Zoo and sometimes movie tickets. I will put some in your mail cubby. Also, I know you do not have a car, so here are some bus passes and a couple of coupons for the Seattle Center. We try to also take the children to the Pacific Science Museum and other field trips. We are here to help empower you and help with the transition. I have a binder of resources and programs that can help you navigate."

I nodded, overwhelmed by their kindness. New Beginnings and the Katherine Booth House were amazing programs. As hard as it was being in a strange city, the advocates and staff cared deeply, and it showed in their work. There were rules. For safety reasons, there was an evening curfew, no drugs or alcohol. There were assigned chores that rotated, and there was a mandatory evening group with childcare provided. I found going to the group difficult at first. It felt like a dysfunctional pajama party as we sat talking about our journey here and used words like protection order, criminal, no contact order and assault. The legalese had become quite familiar to me.

The first few weeks in the new city were made easier by meeting other moms at the park or at the safehouse. We were hiding from Ted. The court had suspended his visitation. The final step was termination of parental rights. This meant no father in Michaela's life and no child support. I had been told many times by the professionals in the case I was too trusting and in denial of Ted's abuse even when I experienced him almost killing me one night. The stalking, the creepy behavior and the rages were intense. It felt so good to be free of that.

While Michaela and I were settling into our new temporary home, my mom had to have a surgery. I could not be there to nurse her. We kept in touch only via letters and the phone. Then, one night Ted's relatives were pounding on her door, yelling and asking for Michaela and me. The neighbor called the police, but they were gone before they arrived. My mom and I spoke, and she decided to move to Seattle. She stayed with me in my safehouse for the holiday and found a senior apartment. My mother loved Seattle.

After the court hearings, she made friends, used her computer that

Collin got her, and became an eBay art seller. She sold many of her paintings. She did art and watched Michaela. She still drank more wine then I thought was good. However, when I brought it up, she would call me the temperance society. It was a sticking point between us that all my family said I should leave alone.

We had a magical, cozy Christmas with my mom there that year. My mom made amazing Yorkshire pudding with standing rib roast. I kept going in and out of vegetarianism. I loved her garlic mashed potatoes and pies. I baked the cookies with Michaela "helping." Michaela made us all gifts with her art supplies.

Over the next two years, good things started happening as my brother Collin won the Rocky Mountain Comedy Competition, launching him from a wedding DJ to standup comedy. Collin was always funny as a child. Each of my brothers had their own unique talents. Collin brought joy and laughter wherever he was. When Michaela spent time with him, he would make her belly-laugh. I have always thought of him as Peter Pan but in a good way, always bringing that childlike wonder to life. He grew into a devoted husband and father. He and my mom had a tight bond but also their own struggles as my mom and dad divorced when he was young. My mother self-medicated with alcohol. I was in and out of the house at seventeen years old and Collin was left alone with my mom at ten years old to navigate the tough times.

In Collin's comedy, he would use truth to heal hard truths through laughter. My mom was so proud as he excelled in his career and even had a Showtime special with many other successes. It was a wonderful but bittersweet time in Seattle. We were far away from cousins and friends, including Andy and Nadine. Andy is Michael's son, and he stayed in the Morro Bay area with his high school sweetheart, Nadine. Tragically, Nadine would die young leaving Andy to raise their daughter Angela as a single dad. The relationship Angela and Andy forged was wonderful and I always knew how proud Michael would be of his son.

While leaving behind all my family and friends was hard, it was even harder to not have proper work since we had our names changed and our lack of secure transportation.

Michaela had been having night terrors since we left Ted. She sometimes shared with me what she was afraid of, and sometimes she did not. I usually just read to her while she colored. Sometimes, we would make hot chocolate and read a book with soft music. At times, she simply could not sleep. I took her to a play therapist. They even had a program for preschoolers to transition into kindergarten. Michaela enjoyed it, and her nightmares lessened. Her pediatrician had wanted to prescribe her sleeping medication, and I refused. I was aghast at how the physicians were willing to medicate children without really knowing the long term effects. Michaela had good nutrition and a consistent bedtime. I had her in a routine: time in nature, play dates and quiet surroundings. Eventually, her nightmares eased.

One challenge we faced was that I needed transportation as our lives were getting busy. I bought a car for $50, and I called it Ivan the Terrible. It smelled like tequila, was rusty, and I had to pour water in it all the time.

Michaela would look down from the car seat and say, "Look, Mama, I see the road."

I realized the rust had gone through. "Ugh," I said.

When Ivan would sputter in protest up the Seattle hills, Michaela would lean forward and say, "Come on, Ivan, you can do it. Come on."

One day, Ivan died a smoky death on Interstate 5.

As the tow truck took us home, Michaela waved bye-bye to Ivan and looked at the truck saying," Mama, I want this car."

Seattle 2000

It was 3am when I woke my daughter up from a deep sleep, and whispered gently, "Come on sweetie, let's go."

"Where, Mama?" she responded.

"The stars, Kiki. You can watch the meteor shower," I smiled and said, "Then we will have hot chocolate and marshmallows."

We put on our warm clothes while Michaela chattered in excitement about the star shower. She was five years old and adorable. She had soft golden curls and big blue eyes.

She said, "Okay, Mama, I got my pack pack."

She had put her toy and stuffed Beanie Babies in it.

I smiled and did not correct her mispronunciation of backpack.

We ran downstairs to the back yard and lay out on the sleeping bag underneath the clear sky and shiny stars. The first stars began to fall in bluish, greenish and reddish colors in a parade every minute. It was better than I could have even imagined. Stars of different colors fell with less frequency as the time passed.

In awe, Michaela asked, "Oh, Mama, they are rainbow stars. Why do they have so many colors?"

"It is because of the Aurora Borealis, or as American's call it the Northern Lights. They reflect the lights from the North Pole and that makes the stars have those colors as they come into the Earth's atmosphere," I explained.

"The North Pole, where Santa Claus lives?" she asked.

I laughed. "Yes, cause, the sun lets out gasses that create the colors in the North Pole."

She giggled. "The sun gets gas, so the sun toots?"

We both laughed harder, and I tickled her. "You are a silly gilly lilly."

As we both got cold, we made our way upstairs, and I made her hot chocolate while she managed the marshmallows.

We snuggled as I read her a book, and she fell asleep only three pages in. The next day, I would let her sleep in after our middle of the night adventure. I kissed her head and remembered my own stargazing.

On the farm, Michael laid out the blanket, and we watched the stars.

Michael pointed out and named constellations, telling me some of the stories attached to the stars.

He taught, "Look, Tara, that is the Big Dipper and there is the Little Dipper."

He pointed his finger, outlining it in the bright Milky Way.

"Michael, what sound do the stars make? Do they sing or talk to each other?" I asked.

Michael chuckled, "I do not know Tara. Maybe they just signal with twinkles like Morse code."

I thought about this and then Michael explained Morse code.

I nodded and wondered what sounds stars could make.

The apartment that Michaela and I had gotten was roomy with a deck overlooking trees. There was a fireplace and washer/dryer combo set. We also had a pool indoors and Jacuzzi outdoors. Michaela had her birthday at the pool, inviting her class from school. A big storm came on that November day, and Michaela, who had helped decorate the play room and filled grab bags, was morose and said, "No one is going to come Mama."

I called around to friends who were valiantly making the trip. The children started arriving, and Michaela was jubilant as everyone dashed to the pool for the warm swim. After everyone went home, we cleaned up and piled into our chair with a blanket as Cleo jumped up to tuck Michaela into bed. She would purr and meow at her fussing to go to sleep. I think Cleo thought Michaela was her kitten. Michaela would giggle when Cleo would push the book from her face at night time. We read *Bun Bun's Birthday* about a rabbit who thought no one loved him on his birthday, but in the end, all his animal friends showed up.

"Mama, I was acting like Bun Bun," She giggled. I nodded.

After that night, Bun Bun was the reference our family used if we thought it would be a lame birthday or party. I loved being a mom. Michaela was an easy child to raise as she was joyful, healthy and inquisitive. People tended to gravitate to her even as she started school because of her kind and calm demeanor. Michaela forged deep ties in Seattle that would last and created a network of good friends.

Washington, D.C. 1993

It was in that deep state of confusion and lack of confidence that was post assault 1993, that I was dating Ted, who was strong and confident.

I was startled to see Ted walking toward me in front of the Capitol again and found myself agreeing to dinner at a local pizza place. Later, he took my hands in his during the whole dinner of pizza slices and beer. His gaze was locked forward, attentive and all-smiling affection. I was smitten by the idea of being smitten. And I don't use words like smitten easily. As he spread red pepper flakes across his meat lovers slice and dabbed grease with a napkin, he talked about his childhood.

I was riveted by his story immediately and the hardships unlike any I had heard. He had been homeless with his disbarred attorney father who had kidnapped him and his two other brothers. They lived in tents, shacks and motel rooms, and traveled via Greyhound bus. His father, he explained, had some sort of mental collapse when he was very young, living in North Dakota with their family.

There are moments in the early part of romantic relationships that through the blur of intimacy, we sense or experience a pull back or pause in bliss. My moment of pause happened at a bagel shop. I received a missed call from him on a Sunday morning. I listened to his routine "Pick me up a garlic bagel with cream cheese and come over" message, his voice deep, commanding, and then came the pause.

A voice that almost sounded outside of myself said urgently, "Get out while you can."

I spun around as I did not hear voices. I sat down waiting for bagels and gathered my thoughts. *Why was I thinking that? Why was I looking for an exit route?*

A domestic violence advocate later said to me in response to my confusion of Ted being so charming and loving at first, "They do not beat you walking down the aisle."

The courtship is that whirlwind romance and deep, quick connected sex-fueled talks, confessions and intimacy that take us ever so methodically to that point where we no longer are even present in our life.

1994

Ted soon invited me to take a weekend trip and, as I discussed the prospect with my friend Stacey, I was hesitant. "I don't know, maybe it's too soon," I said somberly.

"What could possibly be holding you back?" she asked. "You are single, and he adores you. Just let go!"

My misgivings, unbeknownst to Stacey, stemmed from a recent blow-up with Ted after I showed up late to one of our dates. Anger flashed across his face as he shouted at me, "Were you with someone else? Tell me *now*!" I had gotten lost on the freeway and ended up driving toward Maryland and looped around, I tried to explain. After shoving me, he apologized and put his head in his hands.

As the sun descended warmly on the Potomac during our weekend trip, I sat in a rented convertible while we drove toward a Virginia cabin. That night, he fixed me dinner and served me champagne. The next day, the sun was warm as I rested on the deck. Ted brought over a perfect yellow swallowtail butterfly and gently placed it on my knee, careful not to rub the powder from its wings. The irony of his gentleness struck me later as I experienced his horrific brutality to me, and towards others.

Later that spring, a friend told me they could use some volunteers at the Robert F. Kennedy Memorial event at Arlington Cemetery. Excited, I accepted; Robert F. Kennedy was my hero. I asked Ted to accompany me, but he emphatically refused to undergo the compulsory three-day FBI background check.

The day of the memorial, I worked with Kennedy staffers in the VIP tent where the family was sitting. A handsomely chiseled JFK Jr. breezed by with Daryl Hannah. It was a somber but elegant event, and I felt sad Ted had missed it. Later, at the request of Ethel Kennedy, a few of us scraped candle wax that had dripped on the graves.

My friend Shea scraped hard at one tombstone as she said, "Break up with this loser. He wouldn't do the background check. Forget him."

I shook my head, silent.

When I saw Ted later that night, I found myself unable to confront him. Three days later, I received a handwritten thank you note from Ethel Kennedy, but I tucked it away, choosing not to show Ted.

Soon, I received an offer to work on a Governor's race in California, and I almost accepted. Ted kept me up that night, pleading with me to go with him while he managed his Congressman's campaign in the home district of North Dakota. I agreed, and we moved to the frozen tundra of the Midwest. I would not even last a full winter.

The first time he hit me, we had lived in the Midwest together all of two months. The subject of the fight was unremarkable, but the damage to my nose and jaw were not. I was pregnant, we were about to marry and had just gotten a puppy.

There are always red flags when you're in a relationship with a batterer. I always thought I could make it better: I could be on time instead of late. I could be more open emotionally, more organized, more of what Ted wanted. I began losing myself in his constant criticism. Then, when the days of flowers, kindness, and intimacy followed, the bad days faded away.

However, the unease lingered, and soon shifted to panic. One day I found Ted huddled, upset and looking dangerously unstable.

"Take the puppy away *now* and find it a home or I will kill it."

I scooped up the shivering puppy, asking what had happened.

He stared at me blankly. "Don't you understand? I will kill it!" he enunciated every work, his voice rising. "And please have an abortion. I can't stand things that are helpless. I can't be a father, I would just want to kill it."

I felt nauseous. I closed the door, and my heart, staying away from him the rest of the day. It would not be until later that year that I would find out he had killed the cat of a previous girlfriend and committed other unspeakable monstrosities.

One day I called his mother. She listened quietly and said, "Oh, Teddy has problems."

The next day, his mother found a home for the puppy, and I booked a flight home to California. Months later, Ted was fired from his job at a retail company (where he worked after the Congressman's campaign ended) for moral misconduct, hacking into others' email, and some other offense I never knew about. Getting me back became his new project. By showering me with flowers, cards, and endless phone calls as my pregnancy advanced, I finally accepted him back into my life, wanting our child to have her father.

The birth of my daughter was, as it is for many mothers, the highlight and epitome of joy in my life. At that moment, I felt very alive and connected. However, as the events that came after swirled around me, and I tried to catch my breath, my foothold, and stay true to my own dreams, I dissolved somehow into his needs, his demands and the constant tiptoeing around so as not to disturb the rage he had waiting for me, skulking and solid underneath our interactions.

Ted also seemed enamored with Michaela. However, within the next three years, Ted would beat her, threaten her, and commit incredible horrors against both of us.

Our quiet routine was shattered when Ted lost yet another job and was unable to find work.

I immediately took a job with California State Senator Jack O'Connell, but dreaded being away from Michaela as I was still breastfeeding and I wanted time with her.

One day, while I was taking a shower, I heard Michaela's piercing scream. When I ran into the room, Ted handed her to me roughly and sneered, "I shook her. She would not shut up while I was trying to watch TV."

I clung to Michaela, comforting her while I checked for injuries.

In the coming weeks, Ted threatened to kill himself, Michaela and me, if I left. Then, one night in February, he almost succeeded. Another inconsequential fight escalated, and he slammed me against the wall repeatedly. I saw blackness and slid to the floor as he squeezed the air from me, the wood of the futon splintering under his rage. He screamed that he had killed a cat and then I heard Michaela's toddler voice screaming, "Daddy *noooo!*" before I faded into unconsciousness.

I woke up on the floor not sure how long I had been there and immediately wanted to get Michaela but I could not move well. I spent the next few minutes trying to get off the floor, and I walked in to see her sleeping peacefully. Ted lay snoring on his back.

The next morning, the red marks on my body had become bruises. I went to work, hoping the cover-up and scarf would conceal Ted's handprint outlined clearly on my neck. My coworker Lorraine, looked up at me, her eyes registering the source of my pain. I hurried away not wanting attention or a possible scandal.

Lorraine came to my desk and said, "Let's go for a cup of coffee."

We never made it to Starbucks. Instead she walked me into the victim/witness program at the District Attorney's office. Our freedom began with pictures of my face, neck, back, and a restraining order. The divorce began and a custody battle ensued. Ted pled guilty to assault and pled down from a felony to misdemeanor.

It was hopeful to have professionals step into my life to help sort the chaos that ensued when there was intimate partner violence. I stayed in denial a long time as I wanted to keep my family whole. The devastation of acrimonious divorce took its toll financially and emotionally. However, I wanted Michaela to have joy, fun and normal activities in her life. I arranged play dates, beach walks and playground trips. We created beautiful memories like learning to swim, climbing the stairs at the playground, gathering seashells at the coast and creating music.

The first mediation went badly. Judy Selby, the mediator, met with me alone afterward and recommended we be moved out of mediation. Judy met with both of us and reviewed our case.

Judy said, "Tara, I have been doing this work for over twenty years. Ted is dangerous and cold. You need to protect your daughter or the County will."

My life was a series of legal exchanges and stressful nights. However, I sleep deeply. It is a joke among my family and those who know me that I sleep through anything—an earthquake, construction and stalking. My neighbor Lynda met me in my carport one day. I had been hiding out from Ted, sitting and waiting for his temper to cool. He had just thrown Michaela's bottle against the wall in a fit of rage and it shattered, though it was plastic. Michaela had been terrified. I was distracting her looking through a box of toys.

Lynda saw my bruises on my arm. I followed her eyes.

"Oh, I banged myself riding. I have a horse," before she even asked. "Hi, I am Tara."

I extended my hand, she took it and greeted me warmly, telling me about her two children. She lived right next door, so I know she may have heard Ted yelling and the slamming. I felt that shame of wanting to appear as if all was well when it was a scary situation. Our daughters played together and Ari was only one year older. Aaron was their older son and very into technology, already showing signs of being a boy genius. Lynda and I would take the girls on walks to the beach and playground with a group of friends I had from my exercise class. We would have wine and talk on our stoops after our children were asleep, and we formed a deep connection that has lasted a lifetime.

Lynda was going through her own painful separation and worked very hard at her job. She was down to earth with a great sense of humor. She eyed Ted warily, as did many of my friends that came to the house, and got to know us better. Lynda was trying to trust Ted and a couple times, we left our girls with him. However, the violence increased, and she heard Ted get physical and mean to Michaela who was just a toddler. After Ted moved out, Lynda knew about the restraining order. One night at about 2am, she pounded on my door to wake me up.

Lynda said, "I was sitting outside. I could not sleep, and Ted drove into your carport and just sat with his motor running. I called the police."

He had something in his hands. She was so panicked, and I had never seen her that way. Lynda tended to be very laid back and not easily rattled.

"Tara, did you not hear him?" Lynda pleaded.

"No," I answered, "I guess I only hear Michaela." I shook my head wondering what Ted was doing. Lynda then went off to talk to the police, and I showed them my restraining order.

The next day, she and I joked about my deep sleep, and I shared with her how I slept through an earthquake. We laughed, but it was uneasy. The stalking by Ted became so frequent, him creeping in the night around the house, that after I moved out, Lynda put a sign in her window that read "Tara Moved Out." Lynda was fed up with Ted's antics and in a rage about things her children were exposed to because of his behavior.

Ted was on probation and going to an anger-management group. It was Easter Sunday, and he came to see Michaela and I at our new place. It would be the last time we would interact without legal restrictions. He played with Michaela and her Easter basket briefly, then she went down for a nap.

I stood awkwardly wishing that he would just leave, but then he said, "Let's go lie down. I need to lay down now."

What happened next I have not spoken about publicly and rarely privately. Does lightning strike twice? In my case, yes.

Ted had a leather attachment to his belt that snapped. It was a hunting knife. He collected hunting knives. He unholstered it and laid it near the bed. He went to kiss me, and I resisted.

He laughed and said, "Ahh gypsy girl, I miss you."

I was torn with wanting our family to be together and wanting to think Ted had changed. He talked to me earlier about his challenges emotionally and that he was trying. I so wanted to believe him. That's what I wanted. I wanted him to try and make it better. I wanted him to get better. I wanted us to be a family. I sat down on the bed, and he playfully pushed me back, kissing me.

All of a sudden, I felt claustrophobic, and I wanted away. He pushed back and with more aggression. Holding my hands back, he looked to the side. I followed his gaze to the knife. Panicked, I tried to get up.

He said fiercely, "Tara, stop it, or you will wake up Kiki. What is wrong with you? Are you going to let me finish what we started here?"

It seemed as if he thought it was my fault. I looked at him, but he had a vacant stare.

I went limp and he pulled away my dress and underwear as I did not fight. He entered me and I felt a sharp pang, and he began. I lay still and looked out the window at the trees as he moved above me. I was numb. I imagined the leaves sparkling in the sun and drifted away from what he was doing to me.

He left and I was bleeding from the roughness. I thought about what happened all night and went to see Ted's Probation Officer.

Bruce West knew the case and had worked, or somehow was connected, with San Diego Family Resource center and had extensive domestic violence prevention training. I told him about the assaults, threats, what happened to my daughter and the afternoon of Easter. Bruce was silent for a long time.

"It is a probation violation to ignore the restraining order and go to your residence," he reminded me.

"But wait, I let him in and I have made contact with him," somehow defending Ted to Bruce.

Bruce answered slowly and clinically, "You are not restrained. Ted is subject to the law."

Later that week, Bruce called me and asked me to come in to speak to him.

"I am giving you a Tarasoff warning."

"What is that?" I asked.

Quietly he explained the law that was developed to warn potential victims that a person is threatening his or her life and that their life is in immediate danger. I sat quietly.

The Tarasoff case gives social workers the duty to verbally tell the intended victim that there is a foreseeable danger of violence.

I continued to sit and listen.

"I am a mandated reporter, and your life and your daughter's life is in immediate danger, and you need to leave and seek protection." He gave me referrals to the local domestic violence shelter. I left shaken. I packed and left my house that day.

One of the final violent incidents happened to my mother, who was supervising a visit with Michaela. Ted tried to take her, and when my mom protested, he shoved her to the ground. My mother had to have a total hip replacement as a result of the injury.

In 1999, Ted's parental rights were terminated in court due to abuse of his daughter. Later that year, I received news that Ted's DNA was collected by the FBI for two missing women's cases (Kristen Smart and Kristen Modafari) because he was a "person of interest." Ted's profile was that of a sociopath. I only know this because for six hours, on the eve of Thanksgiving, they asked me questions about Ted. They mentioned a particular book, and I knew he had it and read it. That puzzled me, but the FBI does not answer questions, only asks them. I did not know why he was a person of interest. I was only told that he was, and that they needed my cooperation. There were questions that did not make sense to me, but I was far away and starting a new life. I wanted to close the memories of him.

The love I had dreamed of and felt for the father of my child was disintegrated by hostile phone calls, court paperwork, accusations, and domestic violence. There was not even a semblance of who I was or who he was when we met.

Faintly, I saw him in my memory, tender, tall, with his wide open smile, strumming his guitar. I could not reconcile my image of him with the reality that unfolded and the terrible pain he caused both my daughter and me.

In the years that would follow, I functioned. I slept, ate, laughed, cried, worked, watched movies, did laundry, loved my daughter, and still, I felt like I was not really a part of my own creative destiny, not really. I was a ghost in my own life. The grief I felt was not just my own but for my daughter as I so wanted her to have the balance of two parents and a father that cared for her unconditionally.

I listened deeply that day and started my journey to not just understanding the concept of domestic violence on a legal level but a personal one. I also took Judy's referrals and got a therapist for my daughter, who engaged in play therapy. That year was a rollercoaster of events that led to me getting full custody and Ted's parental rights being terminated in 1998.

CHAPTER

11

Boudicca

"It takes skill to win a battle but brains to win a war."
— Boudicca

This chapter is for the audacious women who dare to stand up and speak out. This is for the victim who became a survivor. Remember your power and your right to be here. This chapter is for all the Boudiccas yet to come.

Boudicca was a Celtic warrior Queen for the Iceni tribe in A.D. 60. She led a campaign against the Roman army after she and her daughters were raped and her husband killed by the Romans. After the murder of her husband and the rapes of her daughter and Boudicca, the Romans slaughtered peaceful Druids in the area. Boudicca had enough. She was pissed, "scorch the Earth" angry. In fact, she led, on her two-horse chariot and sword, many successful battles through the year against the Romans. Boudicca almost burned down all of what was then Londinium. Boudicca was fierce and leaned into her rage. Maybe we modern women could learn something from her fierce unending expression of rage that transformed into her power.

In both 1998 and 2019, I decided to take my life back. I decided to fight back with truth as my sword and words as my power. In 2020, I may be politically inconvenient, but it does not change the events of 1993. The stigma and marginalized way I have been portrayed will not last forever. The politically awkward moment does not change my right to stand up and speak my rage that the man running for the most powerful position in the land sexually assaulted me and got away with it.

My need for independence has helped and hurt me. It has helped me try new things, travel to Europe on my own for months and take risks with my career path. However, in our culture, women in traditional intimate relationships are not supposed to demur to men. We live in a patriarchy, so my independence is seen as difficult or non-compliant.

Coming forward with my history about Joe Biden was riddled with landmines meant to silence me. At some point, it is best to come forward and heal. My sanctuary, my relief comes in the form of creative writing, art, nature hikes and horses. I have had many teachers in human and animal form.

I will not always be associated with the men who harmed me. Those experiences do not define me; rather, I define this experience. That is the process of healing, from being a victim to a survivor. I am still on this journey of healing. I channel Boudicca when I feel the daunting power of the machine Joe Biden used to silence and scare me.

I have always sought non-traditional ways of looking at the world and my place in it.

For instance, at nineteen, I met Tara Sutphen, an author, shaman and mystic, who has provided me hope and guidance. She has been one of my greatest teachers. When I contacted her again after my difficult divorce and my daughter was a teen, she offered wisdom.

She said, "Decide to be 'seen' in the world again and step into your destiny."

Years later, I came forward with the secret I hid for so long about Joe Biden.

I called Tara, "Well, I finally took your advice finally and stepped into the world."

Tara Sutphen answered with a chuckle, "Yes, you certainly did. You are seen."

I could hear her beautiful smile through the phone.

We kept in touch as I went through all the media slams and the difficult process of speaking out. Tara helped with the esoteric but also in very practical material ways.

In 1998, I had my sealed name change and sealed social security change. I started a different kind of healing journey that had to do with my daughter. I never thought of myself as a victim. That is a label we are given but not a mantle to hold. Rather, I saw myself as just another human being going through the same unfortunate domestic violence that three out of five American women experience. The shocking statistic has remained static for decades even with the Violence Against Women Act. I remember reading the briefings and taking notes at hearings about these issues when I lived in Washington, D.C.

On the way to the courthouse in 1999, I was somber.

The advocate in the seat next to me said, "Have you thought of a name?"

I looked at the moody Seattle skyline racing by as we descended into downtown in the car.

I sighed, "I don't know."

I thumbed through the baby name book. My mother had planned to call me Lara. However, my father wanted a different name so she chose Tara. I see the name.

Alexandra. I think. That is it. No one would fuck with Alexandra. Alexandra sounded bad ass. For Michaela, I was sad as I named her after my brother Michael, and her middle name Rosalie was after my Aunt who was killed in a car accident.

McCabe came from an old family name that no one knew. Inside the courthouse the judge was seriously considering the documents and reviewed Michaela's paperwork that had Ted's termination of parental rights. He lowered his glasses and said slowly that it was granted. He reminded me to not link my old identity with my new one, and that was court ordered. I agreed. I breathed for the first time.

My mood shifted to happiness when my ex-boyfriend from years before, Fábe, sent Cleo, my cat, to me under an assumed name. Also, my mother was allowed to come into the New Beginnings housing program with me. Michaela was making friends and happy to see her Nana. We were free. I just needed our new social security numbers.

On December 10th, 1998, I woke up in my new apartment furnished by Ikea with my daughter and mom there. My cat was curled in the Ikea rocking chair. I threw on my sweats to check the mail and saw the new cards. I was ecstatic and ran to the advocate's office to tell her. People in the office were crying, and then looked at me. I hesitantly asked what was wrong.

"Melanie and Carli were shot and killed yesterday at the visitation center."

I was stunned. I had just seen Melanie, but she was leaving as I was coming in. Michaela had played with Carli a couple of times. Michaela brushed her hair and played with the toys with her in the waiting area. The judge had ordered the visitation since the monitor had written how positive his interactions were with Carli. He gave her a little stuffed bear. She died holding the stuffed toy he had given her, as when he shot them both at point blank range after the visit. Melanie had plans and a new job. It was reported she was happy and free for the first time. On that dark cold night, it all ended. I told Michaela about Carli as best I could when she saw everyone crying.

Michaela lifted her chin and said, "Oh, her mean daddy found her."

She said this matter of fact, and it broke my heart. Her memories of Ted caused her nightmares, and whatever he did at the visits with her left bruises and trauma. The professionals involved, including a medical doctor, made police reports and recommended his parental rights be terminated. Michaela had play therapy, and her night terrors eventually eased. It bothered me that the presence of violent men was becoming the norm and not a surprise to Michaela. In my life, my brothers were always kind and gentle, including my stepbrothers. My father was abusive, but I had so many other positive male figures in my life. I hoped Michaela would have that too, and that she would know kind and gentle men.

However, on this day, December 10th, instead of celebrating my new identity and freedom, I lit a candle and said a prayer for Melanie Edwards and her little girl Carli, who tried their best to start again but could not survive.

Later that year, a young woman staying at New Beginnings called the hotline to say she wanted to exit the shelter to go to a party. The advocates on the line were trained to "empower" women. They said it was up to her but discussed the risk and why she was there. She was twenty-one years old and missed her friends. She was in a shelter with rules and curfews, and she wanted freedom. She left her son with a sitter and went. She never came back. Her ex-boyfriend found her at the party and killed her. He wrapped her body in a rug and threw it in a ditch. His father was a police officer and well respected in the community.

She had a will that directed care for her son to go to her parents in another state.

What young twenty-one-year-old leaves a will? I had wondered. This one did, and her ex-boyfriend's parents tried for custody, but could not get it due to the will. There were vigils and a call to address domestic violence. Then, the world moved on and forgot.

We would have a "group" at the shelter, it was like an odd tragic pajama party. I tolerated it, but never felt it got to the point where healing could begin. I tended to leave first thing in the morning. I would take care of things all day with Michaela, taking her to parks and playgrounds, meeting families with none of the issues to which we were in proximity. While I was grateful for the housing and resources, I wanted my daughter to have peace and know joy.

I quickly secured work and housing. Michaela thrived and loved having our own space. She said, "Oh, Mama, it's so nice without all the people."

She was a quieter person and, as the only child, she appreciated peace. This significant movement forward, and the work I did with other survivors, led to a rewarding part of my life. In 2004, I graduated from law school. We had a big celebration with friends and family. My brother had a comedy show and there was such joy that weekend. My daughter was happy and had her best friends, her music lessons, and art with Nana. We would go to waterfalls and walk among the old forests outside of Seattle. We would take ferries and have picnics with her group of friends. Life broke open, and we were able to chase rainbows instead of holding back tears. It was a time of laughter and adventures.

I remember the time Michaela realized she could read a book on her own and how excited she was, like riding her scooter or bike. I treasured every day with her and often let other things go to the wayside, like dating, or law school, because time with her was magical and fleeting. I knew in a blink of an eye it would be gone. Healing comes in all forms, and sometimes the coo of a child, a purr of your cat, or a warm bath free of stress. It is when you can sleep unaware and unafraid. Freedom is when you can let go of the rage and then experience the sweet taste of survival. Forgive yourself and you will find forgiving others comes in its own time. I treasured those years, especially because I had seen or been near death. My brother Michael, and those women who were killed, taught me not to fear death but to embrace life. Their deaths were a stern reminder of the moments slipping by.

Since coming forward in 2019, I have garnered many new friends, even with Covid-19 lockdowns. I met some amazing people in person and on the phone. I had supporters devote so much energy and love to me, it inspired me. The Team Tara as they call themselves started forming in earnest after the craven *NYT* piece dropped. A graduate student, Kait, found the Larry King call. CNN had it and was willing to charge reporters for it, and they never aired it. Ryan Grim and Rich McHugh broke the story with the help from Kait who cared. I connected with her to thank her and we remained in contact. She helped me all summer as I was being attacked legally and having my reputation destroyed. Avalon Clare, who I call my Aaron Rodgers (I am ever the Green Bay Packer cheesehead fan), has worked tirelessly to help me with everything from gathering a team of people, creating a website and helping with the book by donating her time for the book cover design. Her boyfriend Angus graciously helped where he could, and we had many bets regarding the Packers. 2020, even the shitshow that it is, will hopefully bring the Packers to the Super Bowl.

I have had some surreal days. One morning, I received a call from Anita Hill. She was kind and wise with words of comfort for what I was going through. It was not about believing me or politics but rather the intense scrutiny and negative media. The conversation was brief but intense, and I wished I had had coffee first. Later that day, I talked with Sean Hannity. He was kind and understood the difficult position I was in trying to come forward in such a hostile environment.

As the days filled with challenges and difficulties, I was grateful for the people showing up to ease my suffering. It made me feel free of all the confinement that comes with silence. A symbol of freedom for me has always been the horse. I have had a lifelong fascination with horses and their power of healing.

When I was in my twenties, my mother and my boyfriend, Fábe, were watching me with my horse. I walked up to them as my mom said, "Give her a lot of space, she is like that horse—she needs no fences and space to run."

She smiled. Fábe laughed and said he already knew that about me. My mother knew my need for open spaces mentally and physically. It was many years ago, but my mom was astute in her understanding of my almost compulsion for freedom of mind and spirit. I did not enjoy walls at work or in relationships. One of my spirit animals has always been the horse.

My love for horses started as a small child. I have owned several horses throughout my life. Charm is my latest horse that I adopted. He lives up to his name. I always have believed horses love to be in a herd and free to run. My horse lives on acres with a herd, and he is now the leader. He is proud and intelligent. He loves to grab my hat, and he plays soccer with me. I have experienced great healing being with my horse.

I have always been passionate about anti-slaughter legislation. During my internship with Panetta, and the cruel round ups of our wild horses, I was determined to try to work on it. All that passed was a bipartisan bill that allowed safe transport to slaughter, but not the end of slaughter. I will continue to use whatever platform I can to educate people about the useless brutality of horse slaughter.

During the time I was coming forward in 2020 with my full history, at one ranch, I went to the other women when I saw that the articles about me were negative. They would turn their backs and not speak to me when they saw me. It became so cruel that the owner of the ranch yelled at them when she saw it happening. At the same time, a bottom-feeder made false accusations against me when she saw my story in the media. Her hatred of me for coming forward was cruel and senseless. She would often go on vitriolic attacks towards certain people and intimidate them with ruining them. She used social media to say horrible things and to try to "take Charm for America." I filed a Cease and Desist order, which she ignored. I decided to leave the bottom-feeder alone with one of her own ugly lies, and I moved on mentally. Meanwhile, someone else on social media threatened to kill my cats and my daughter. The trolls screamed and typed their vile views.

I created a safety plan for my horse. I made a police report, and the ranch owner said no way would anyone take my horse. Charm remained blissfully unaware of all this drama, but he did sense my moods, and he would act out when he saw my tenseness. Horses can be our greatest mirrors and greatest teachers. They demand we come correct and deal with our shadows on our own time. As my brother Collin once said to me, "Pay attention. This is your life."

I engaged in talk therapy and non-traditional approaches, such as mindfulness meditation yoga and art, to heal PTSD and trauma. I mostly loved my sessions with Tara Sutphen that were in the moment but also looking onward. Talk therapy was all about looking back. I found the best ways to integrate was by integrating my past to my future with all these approaches, and through creative writing. Also, nature, for me, has always been the greatest healer. I feel connected to why I am here when I am deep in an ocean or walking in the mountains. The smell of my horse and feel of his mane has always brought instant peace. Sitting with my cat having tea in the morning is calming. Walking along the beach and watching dolphins leap teaches us that there is joy bounding through the ocean.

One of the most important parts of healing is creating that transformation from victim to survivor. After the media attacks on my character it became clear to me that part of my future life's work would be to forge a path for others with similar stories to be able to do so with more dignity and less fear. One of the main ways to create this change is to examine the media bias I experienced just because the person that assaulted me was a Democrat. In order for rape culture to truly change, we have to change collectively the way we approach this. Rape is an uncomfortable subject. However, through understanding and compassion we can bring healing rather than more pain and trauma.

The act of coming forward will bring the threats and hardships, but it shouldn't be that hard to tell the truth. I do not regret one minute of the past two years. I did lose a great deal, but I gained more freedom. My greatest wish is for the next survivor to know compassion and understanding coming forward. My hope is that, through compassion, I can heal that Boudicca part of me that wants a reckoning, and I can truly know the peace of forgiveness. I am not in that place yet. However, I am circling for a landing to a deeper understanding and that is the path to forgiveness. I have found that for me the art of survival is the subtle ability to adapt and move forward. I know deep inside me is the strength and courage of Boudicca.

RESOURCES

If you, or someone you know, needs help fighting domestic abuse, has been sexually harassed or worse, here are some recommended resources.

Echo Training

We provide trauma & resilience training for families, communities, professionals and organizations. We draw on the latest scientific research on trauma as well as emotional regulation techniques and nonviolent communication to empower survivors and educate those who support them.

www.echotraining.org

Hire Survivors Hollywood

Hire Survivors Hollywood aims to raise support for survivors of sexual violence within the entertainment industry by encouraging those in positions of power to pledge to Hire Survivors and Silence Breakers.

https://hiresurvivorshollywood.org

Voices In Action

Voices in Action is a survivor-founded and led 501(c)3 nonprofit fighting to change the culture of sexual misconduct and violence through a holistic and innovative set of services and programming that work to protect and prevent incidents of abuse, provide advocacy and support to victims, empower survivors, uncover serial perpetrators, and hold abusers accountable for their actions.

https://voicesinaction.org

King County Sexual Assault Resource Center

King County Sexual Assault Resource Center's (KCSARC's) purpose is to alleviate, as much as possible, the trauma of sexual assault for victims and their families. Our mission is to give voice to victims, their families, and the community; create change in beliefs, attitudes, and behaviors about violence; and instill courage for people to speak out about sexual assault.

https://www.kcsarc.org

Washington State Coalition Against Domestic Violence

Founded in 1990 by survivors and their allies, we are a non-profit 501(c)3 network of domestic violence programs. Our membership works tirelessly across the state to help survivors towards safety and freedom. Our work includes visionary leadership, supporting our member programs, and engaging the public to play a role in ending domestic and sexual violence.

https://wscadv.org

Ryther Child Center

Helping children, youth, young adults, and their families find their path to healing and hope is at the core of our work. We can only achieve this by striving for excellence and providing an array of services that are needed and wanted by the community we serve. As an agency, we are focused on evidence-based practices, we have enhanced the quality and effectiveness of our work by implementing a trauma care model – Attachment, Regulation, and Competency (ARC). We are continuing to expand our service array and locations where we provide services, with therapists in more schools and social service agencies. As we expand our services to serve more than 800 children, youth and young adults each month – regardless of payer, gender identity, sexual orientation, race or ethnicity or place of origin – we do so with the intention that we would want our own families to use these services should they need them.

https://www.ryther.org

National Sexual Violence Resource Center

The NSVRC's mission is to provide leadership in preventing and responding to sexual violence through collaboration, sharing and creating resources, and promoting research.

https://www.nsvrc.org

New Beginnings

Founded in 1976, New Beginnings' mission is to empower survivors and mobilize community awareness and action to end domestic violence. We are the only full service agency in Seattle whose primary mission is to serve domestic violence survivors. With over 40 years of established history, New Beginnings has become a leading force in the movement to end domestic violence and has grown to include a full range of services for survivors. On average, New Beginnings serves over 10,000 women, children, and men each year.

https://www.newbegin.org

Network For Victim Recovery DC

Starting in 2012, NVRDC founders sought to create an organization dedicated to providing a seamless network of referrals and services to all D.C. crime victims. Network for Victim Recovery of DC empowers victims of all crimes to achieve survivor-defined justice through a collaborative continuum of advocacy, case management and legal services.

https://www.nvrdc.org

Planet 9

Planet 9 takes you on a very special journey. I am not trying to be a pop star, I will not be performing this album. By using my knowledge of cinema sound design, I carefully created the sounds and words for a better place, an unknown world in our own mind that we can all travel to. Planet 9 is an artistic endeavor that I hope will help others meditate in a unique way. Let go, come to Planet 9.

https://www.rosemcgowan.com

Tara Reade

Tara Reade was born in Monterey California. She spent the younger part of her childhood in the north woods of Wisconsin. Later, she lived in Georgia and California. Tara always loved horses, being in nature, and was an avid skier.

She studied classical theatre and performed in many Shakespeare plays throughout her life. As a teenager, Tara moved to California and was a professional model and actress. She acted in such productions as, *The Days and Nights of Molly Dodd*, *Highway to Heaven* and played a dancer in the film *La Bamba*.

Tara then became a political operative working on a congressional race as a Field Manager and Intern for Leon Panetta. Tara worked on an animal advocacy issue that became a law, coordinating the legislative briefings. She also became a staffer for then Senator Joseph Biden. After some time, Tara moved back to California with her daughter Michaela, and worked for State Senator Jack O'Connell.

In 1998, Tara and her daughter moved to Seattle Washington. As a survivor of domestic violence Tara wanted to advocate for other women so she graduated from law school in 2004. Tara worked as a Victim Advocate for the King County Prosecutor's Office. Tara is a certified FLETC Homeland Security Domestic Violence Prevention Instructor. Over the years, she worked for several nonprofits to support domestic violence victims. Tara used her training and work experience to become an Expert Witness for Domestic Violence Court and presented training in her community of Monterey. Tara also worked as an Executive Director for an animal rescue.

Tara loves creative writing. She has written and published several articles and poems throughout her life. In 2019, she started the novel, *The Last Snow Tiger* due to come out in 2021. Tara continues to advocate for animals and lives with her rescued cats and adopted horse, Charm.

Published by

TVGUESTPERT PUBLISHING

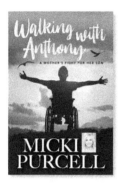

MICKI PURCELL
Walking With Anthony: A Mother's Fight For Her Son
Hardcover $22.95
Kindle: $9.99

JACK H. HARRIS
Father of the Blob: The Making of a Monster Smash and Other Hollywood Tales
Paperback: $16.95
Kindle/Nook: $9.99

New York Times Best Seller
CHRISTY WHITMAN
The Art of Having It All: A Woman's Guide to Unlimited Abundance
Paperback: $16.95
Kindle/Nook: $9.99
Audible Book: $13.00

IAN WINER
Ubiquitous Relativity: My Truth is Not the Truth
Paperback: $16.95
Kindle: $9.99

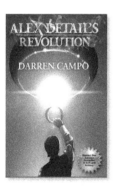

DARREN CAMPO
Alex Detail's Revolution
Paperback: $9.95
Hardcover: $22.95
Kindle: $9.15

DARREN CAMPO
Alex Detail's Rebellion
Hardcover: $22.95
Kindle: $9.99

DARREN CAMPO
Disappearing Spell: Generationist Files: Book 1
Kindle: $2.99

DARREN CAMPO
Stingers
Paperback: $9.99
Kindle: $9.99

TVGuestpert Publishing
11664 National Blvd, #345
Los Angeles, CA. 90064
310-584-1504
www.TVGPublishing.com

JOANNA DODD MASSEY
Culture Shock: Surviving Five Generations in One Workplace
Paperback: $16.95
Kindle/Nook: $9.99

JACQUIE JORDAN AND SHANNON O'DOWD
*The Ultimate On-Camera Guidebook: Hosts*Experts*Influencers*
Paperback: $16.95
Kindle: $9.99

JACQUIE JORDAN
Heartfelt Marketing: Allowing the Universe to Be Your Business Partner
Paperback: $15.95
Kindle: $9.99
Audible: $9.95

JACQUIE JORDAN
Get on TV! The Insider's Guide to Pitching the Producers and Promoting Yourself
Published by Sourcebooks
Paperback: $14.95
Kindle: $9.99
Nook: $14.95

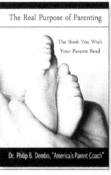

GAYANI DESILVA, MD
A Psychiatrist's Guide: Helping Parents Reach Their Depressed Tween
Paperback: $16.95
Kindle: $9.99

GAYANI DESILVA, MD
A Psychiatrist's Guide: Stop Teen Addiction Before It Starts
Paperback: $16.95
Kindle: $9.99
Audible: $14.95

DR. PHILIP DEMBO
The Real Purpose of Parenting: The Book You Wish Your Parents Read
Paperback: $15.95
Kindle: $9.99
Audible: $23.95

EVE MICHAELS
Dress Code: Ending Fashion Anarchy
Paperback: $15.95
Kindle/Nook: $9.99
Audible Book: $17.95

LEFT OUT: WHEN THE TRUTH DOESN'T FIT IN

CPSIA information can be obtained
at www.ICGtesting.com
Printed in the USA
LVHW081524171222
735438LV00022B/1030/J